macOS Sonoma User Guide

A Complete Manual to Unlock the Full Potential of Your MacBook and iMacs from Desktop Customization to Troubleshooting Tips and Tricks

Patrick B. Hurtado

© Copyrights 2023 – Patrick B. Hurtado

All rights reserved.

This book's contents may not be reproduced, duplicated, or transmitted without direct written permission from the author or publisher. No blame or legal responsibility will be held against the publisher or author for any damages, reparations, or monetary loss due to the information contained in this book. Whether directly or indirectly.

Disclaimer Notice:

Please note that the information within this document is for educational and entertainment purposes only. All efforts have been made to present reliable and complete information. However, no warranties of any kind are implied or declared. This book is an independent publication and is not endorsed or authorized by Apple Inc. We are not affiliated with Apple, and the information provided in this book is based on our research.

While every effort has been made to ensure the accuracy and relevance of the content, technology and software can change rapidly. The author and publisher are not responsible for any errors, omissions, or any adverse consequences resulting from the use of the information provided in this book. Readers are encouraged to consult official documentation, seek professional advice, and exercise due diligence when applying the concepts and instructions discussed herein.

Table of Contents

Table of Contents iii

Introduction vii
    New Desktop Wallpaper Features vii
    Tidy Up Your Desktop viii
    Turning Websites into Web Apps viii
    Stickers and Message Effects ix
    Streamlined PDF Form Filling ix
    Enhanced Siri Integration x
    Presenter Overlay: A New Meeting Experience x
    Saying Goodbye to Mouse Acceleration xi
    iCloud Plus Plans xi
    Personal Voice xii
    Using Desktop Widgets xii

Chapter 1: Apple's Latest Release: Mac OS Sonoma 1
    Dynamic Wallpapers 2
    Widgets on Your Desktop 3
    Hide Items on Desktop 6
    Desktop Interaction: 'Click Wallpaper to Reveal Desktop' 7
    System-Wide Typing Enhancements 8
    Improved Dictation 9
    Enhanced PDF Editing in Notes 10
    Enhanced Video Calls 12
    Safari and Web Applications 14
    Advanced Privacy Controls 17
    Game Mode 18
    Screen Time Enhancements 19

Accessibility and Live Captions *21*

App Improvements *23*

Chapter 2: Mac Basics for Beginners **28**

Overview of Mac Interface *31*

System Settings *35*

The Finder *36*

Useful Shortcuts *39*

Zooming Systemwide *40*

Screenshot Capture *40*

File Renaming *41*

Image Size Conversion *42*

Chapter 3: A Windows User's Guide to Mac Basics **44**

Spotlight *46*

Settings *49*

Finder *51*

Working with Multiple Finder Windows *55*

Keyboard Shortcuts on Mac *56*

Managing Windows *57*

Using Safari *57*

Installing Applications on Mac *59*

Managing Dock *60*

Closing Applications *61*

Chapter 4: Stage Manager and Mission Control **63**

Introducing Stage Manager *63*

Mission Control *66*

Mastering Your Trackpad *68*

Chapter 5: Mastering macOS: Essential Mac Getting Started Tips **70**

Adjust Tracking Speed *70*

Enable Tap to Click... *70*

Enable Three-Finger Drag... *71*

Adjust Mouse Tracking Speed *71*

Enable Secondary Click (Right-Click) for Magic Mouse *71*

Configure Swipe Between Pages for Magic Mouse *72*

Set Up Apple Watch Unlock.. *72*

Setting Up Hot Corners *73*

Enabling Keyboard Navigation *74*

Customizing Your Computer Name... *74*

Quick Access to Sound Settings *75*

Removing Spotlight from the Menu Bar.. *75*

Configuring Finder Window Defaults *75*

Configuring the Finder Sidebar... *76*

Keeping Folders on Top... *77*

Customizing Search Behavior *77*

Enabling the Status Bar... *78*

Customizing Screenshots.. *78*

Using Stacks for a Tidy Desktop *80*

Customizing Safari Start Page *81*

Customizing the Dock... *82*

Chapter 6: Important Settings You Need to Change **85**

Change Your Wallpaper for Cool Animation... *85*

Add Widgets to Your Desktop.. *86*

Change Desktop Interaction Behavior.. *86*

Set Up Web Applications *87*

Manage Game Mode *87*

Enable Auto-Switching for AirPods... *88*

Turn Off Predictive Text 88

Customize Safari Profiles 88

Clean Up Verification Codes 89

Share Passwords with Family 89

Adjust Video Effects for Video Calls 90

Configure 'Hey Siri' Settings 91

Chapter 7: MacBook Pro Beginners Guide 92

Some important settings 94

Applications 95

Hot corners 100

Notification Center Customization 101

Stage Manager for Application Organization 102

Safari and Finder Tabs 103

How to Screen Record on Mac 104

Chapter 8: Troubleshooting 106

macOS Sonoma Desktop Widgets Not Working on Mac 106

MacBook Camera Not Working 107

macOS Sonoma Not Updating 108

macOS Sonoma Bluetooth Issues 110

macOS Sonoma Draining Your Battery 113

No Internet After Upgrade 115

Wi-Fi Problems on macOS Sonoma 116

MacBook Screen Flickering 119

Fixing Keyboard and Trackpad Issues on MacBook Pro 121

Most Common macOS Sonoma Issues and Fixes 124

Conclusion 128

Introduction

Mac OS Sonoma is here, and it's not just about pretty visuals like animated screen savers and widgets. We'll dive into the practical features that can simplify your daily life.

New Desktop Wallpaper Features

Apple's Sonoma brings an interesting tweak to your desktop wallpaper. By default, you can now "click wallpaper to reveal desktop." But this can sometimes be a little intrusive when you accidentally activate it. To make this feature less pesky, you can restrict it to when you're using the "stage manager." You can adjust this setting in 'Desktop and Dock' under System Preferences.

Tidy Up Your Desktop

Another new addition is the ability to hide everything on your desktop. No more fumbling around with separate apps for this task; it's integrated into Mac OS Sonoma. However, bear in mind that when you hide everything, you can no longer right-click on the desktop.

Turning Websites into Web Apps

You can transform any website into a web app for quick and easy access. Say goodbye to sifting through your browser tabs. Just visit the desired URL, click on the share button, and select 'add to Dock.' Next time you open the app, you'll be amazed by how speedy and clean the experience is.

Compatibility Check

Before you take the plunge into Mac OS Sonoma, ensure your Mac is compatible. Apple provides a handy list on their website.

New Desktop Right-Click Options

When you right-click on your desktop, you'll notice a fresh option, 'import from iPhone,' and the convenient 'scan documents' feature. Scanning and saving documents is now a breeze and can be a real time-saver.

Stickers and Message Effects

In Messages, you can now enjoy new stickers, similar to those on iOS 17. Create your own stickers and share them with friends for fun reactions. It's a delightful addition.

Streamlined PDF Form Filling

Filling out PDF forms in Preview has become much more efficient. The 'form filler toolbar' populates empty fields automatically, saving you the hassle of manually adding text fields. Just tab through the fields, and you're done in no time.

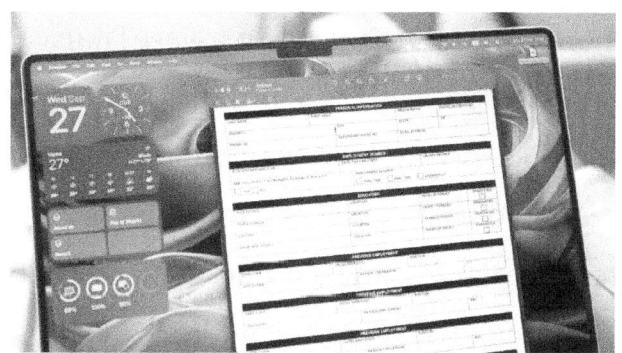

Enhanced Siri Integration

Siri is no longer just for your iPhone. You can now harness the power of Siri on your Mac. Head to Siri and Spotlight in settings, and you'll find options to activate 'Hey Siri' or simply 'Siri.' It's impressively fast and responsive.

Presenter Overlay: A New Meeting Experience

In Sonoma, Apple introduces 'Presenter Overlay,' a feature that's a game-changer for virtual meetings. During FaceTime calls or Zoom meetings, you can now float your video feed over your shared screen, allowing you to maintain a professional appearance even if your surroundings are less than ideal. To activate this feature, simply share your screen and head to the camera icon in the menu bar to toggle on 'Presenter Overlay.'

An intriguing aspect is how well this works when using your iPhone as a camera. During a FaceTime call using the iPhone 15 Pro and the continuity camera setting, Presenter Mode proves highly functional and allows you to customize your appearance. You can choose a small Presenter Overlay or a large one, depending on your preference. The quality of the iPhone 15 camera is outstanding when combined with your laptop.

Saying Goodbye to Mouse Acceleration

For gamers and enthusiasts, there's a significant change. Sonoma introduces the ability to disable mouse acceleration in the settings, a long-awaited feature. No more need for complex terminal commands. Mouse acceleration adjusts the cursor's speed based on your mouse movement, and disabling it can be particularly useful for gamers who want precise control.

iCloud Plus Plans

For those deeply ingrained in the Apple ecosystem, the introduction of iCloud Plus plans is worth mentioning. While not exclusive to Sonoma, it's a concurrent addition. Previously, the largest iCloud plan was 2 TB. Now, you can choose from 2 TB, 6 TB, and even 12 TB plans. This expansion is especially beneficial if you're managing Android devices but rely on a Mac as your primary laptop.

Personal Voice

Exploring accessibility features, you'll discover 'Personal Voice.' This feature allows you to generate text-to-speech using AI based on your own voice. Although this feature was previously showcased in iPhone videos, it's now integrated into Sonoma. To set it up, find a quiet environment with minimal reverb and spare at least 15 minutes to read 150 phrases. The end result is a personalized voice generator that mimics your speech patterns.

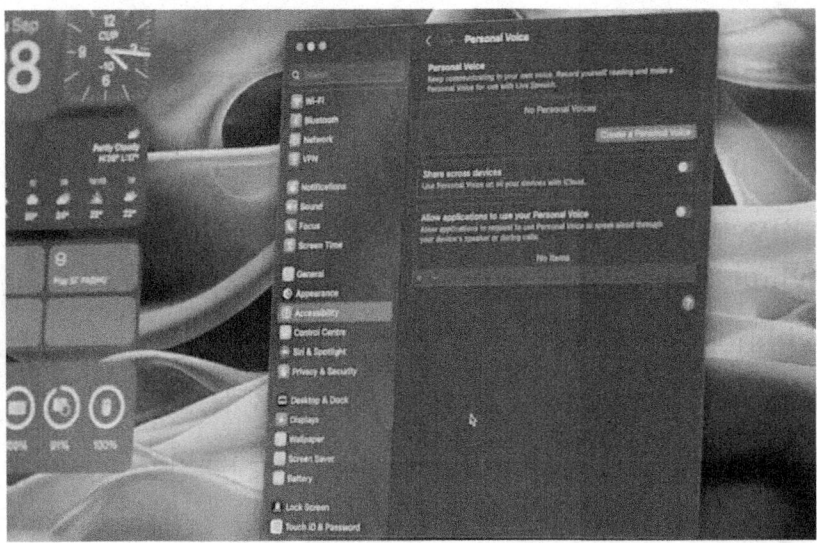

Using Desktop Widgets

One exciting addition is the ability to use widgets on your Mac desktop. However, distinguishing between iPhone widgets and Mac widgets can sometimes be confusing. iPhone widgets often prompt you to open the associated app on your phone. While this is a nifty feature, it may require some getting used to.

- A quick tip for Mac users: You can efficiently quit apps on the fly by pressing **Command + Q** or using **Command + Tab**. This can help you declutter your workspace and streamline your multitasking.

In this book, you will learn valuable insights into Mac OS Sonoma to make the most of your updated Mac experience, enhancing productivity and efficiency.

Let's get started!

Chapter 1: Apple's Latest Release: Mac OS Sonoma

In this chapter, we'll dive into the over 100 brand-new features and changes that Mac OS Sonoma brings to the table. Let's start by exploring the first thing you'll encounter after installing this update: the impressive new lock screen.

Translucent Time and Dates

Upon entering the lock screen, you'll immediately notice the more translucent time and date display at the top. The visual improvements are a subtle yet refreshing touch.

User and Password Input

At the bottom of the lock screen, you'll find the user and password input fields. This is also where you can select different users, consolidating user management in one location. As you interact with the lock screen, you'll observe the background subtly moving.

Dynamic Wallpapers

With Mac OS Sonoma, your screensavers seamlessly transition into wallpapers, providing a more dynamic visual experience. Additionally, there's a wide selection of wallpapers, including landscape, cityscape, underwater, Earth, and even Aerial screensavers from Apple TV.

Wallpaper Customization

- To customize your wallpaper, visit the **wallpaper settings**.

Notably, some wallpapers require individual downloads, and you can monitor the download progress. You'll also have the option to add photos or entire folders/albums as wallpapers.

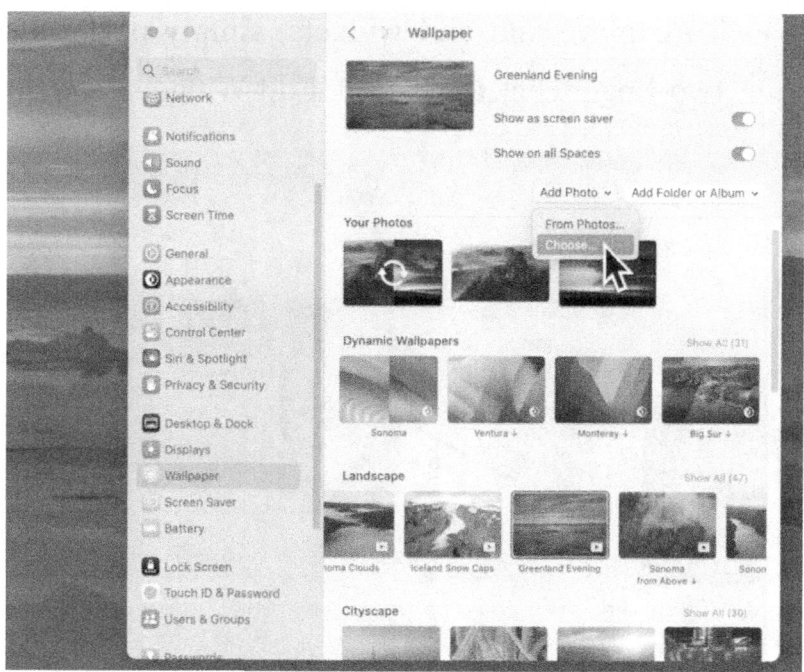

Widgets on Your Desktop

A significant enhancement in Mac OS Sonoma is the inclusion of widgets on your desktop. Previously confined to the notification center, you can now place widgets directly on your desktop.

You can rearrange widgets to suit your preferences, providing a considerable degree of customization. While some constraints exist, you have the freedom to position widgets as you like.

Accessing Widgets

- To explore and add widgets, simply perform a two-finger click and select 'Edit Widgets.'

A widget tray will appear, offering a variety of widgets for your desktop.

Cross-Device Compatibility

Widgets on Mac OS Sonoma make use of **continuity**, allowing you to utilize widgets from your other Apple devices, like your iPhone or iPad. This cross-device integration extends to applications installed on those devices.

Dynamic Widgets

Widgets on your desktop are dynamic, enabling you to interact with them directly. For example, you can mark off items on a grocery list widget, even when you're in another application. This functionality adds a layer of convenience to your desktop experience.

Widget Appearance Customization

You can adjust the appearance of widgets to your liking. Access the widget settings in the desktop and Dock preferences, where you can choose between monochrome and full-color styles. These settings offer versatility in widget aesthetics.

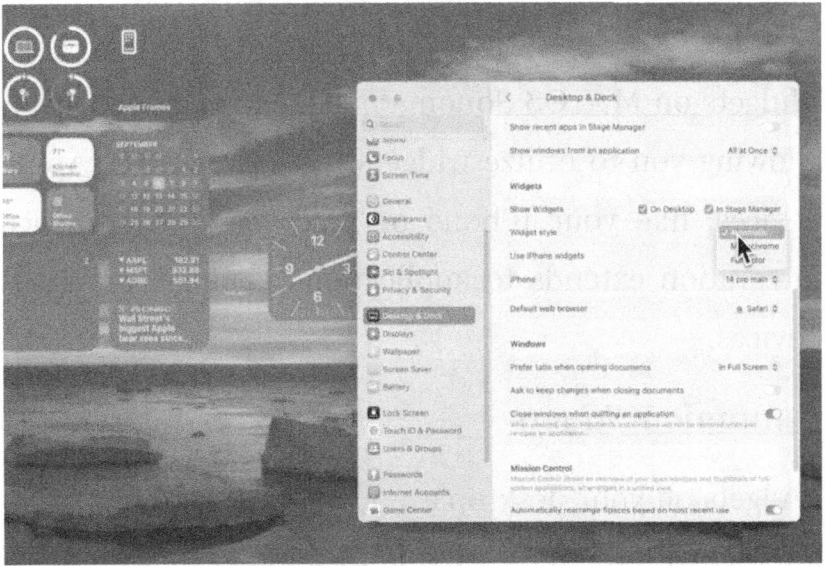

Size Customization

One standout feature of Mac OS Sonoma is the ability to change widget sizes on the fly without the need to create new widgets. This flexibility streamlines the customization process.

Hide Items on Desktop

Under the desktop and **Dock settings**, you'll find the 'Desktop and Stage Manager' section. A standout feature here is the ability to control what appears on your desktop. You can choose to display or hide items, which refers to the elements on your desktop. This feature eliminates the need for third-party apps or manual organization to declutter your desktop.

Widget Customization

Continuing with widgets, you can further enhance your desktop experience. The option to turn off widgets 'on desktop' and display them only in Stage Manager allows you to maintain a clean desktop when needed. This flexible approach allows you to enjoy widgets while working in the Stage Manager, streamlining your desktop appearance.

Stage Manager Settings

The Stage Manager itself offers additional customization. You can toggle a 'Stage Manager' kill switch and specify whether you want to 'show recent apps in Stage Manager' or display 'windows from an application one at a time or all at once.' These settings provide more control over your Stage Manager experience, allowing you to tailor it to your preferences.

Desktop Interaction: 'Click Wallpaper to Reveal Desktop'

A unique feature in Mac OS Sonoma is the controversial 'Click Wallpaper to Reveal Desktop' option. When set to 'always,' this feature hides all active windows when you click on the desktop, revealing your widgets, icons, and saved files. Click again to restore the previous view. This feature can be useful for quickly accessing your desktop content, though opinions on its utility may vary.

System-Wide Typing Enhancements

Typing Indicator

A system-wide typing indicator is a prominent addition in Mac OS Sonoma. The indicator, seen in apps like Reminders and Notes, is more noticeable with its thicker, application-matching colors. This indicator helps you identify typing activity across various apps.

Caps Lock Indicator

For added convenience, the Caps Lock indicator is now present. It subtly informs you of Caps Lock activation when you stop typing, ensuring you're aware of your keyboard's status, particularly when entering passwords.

Predictive Text and Autocorrect Improvements

Mac OS Sonoma introduces predictive text, which suggests words as you type. It adapts over time as it learns your typing patterns. While it can be a time-saver, you have the flexibility to disable this feature in system settings under 'show inline predictive text.'

Autocorrect Enhancement

Autocorrect receives a substantial upgrade, akin to iOS and iPad OS 17. It provides improved suggestions for correcting mistyped words. You now have the option to revert to your original input rather than accepting the autocorrected word.

Improved Dictation

In Mac OS Sonoma, dictation capabilities have been enhanced. You can now dictate text, switch to typing, and then return to dictation without pressing the dictate button multiple times. This new feature streamlines the dictation process, making it more user-friendly.

Notably, dictation accuracy has improved in Mac OS Sonoma. Users can expect more precise transcriptions compared to Mac OS Ventura. These system-wide enhancements make Mac OS Sonoma a user-centric and versatile operating system, with features that simplify desktop management, typing, and dictation tasks while enhancing overall user experience.

Enhanced PDF Editing in Notes

Mac OS Sonoma introduces a range of improvements to PDF handling within the Notes application, making it more versatile for managing your documents.

PDF Import and Display

To begin with, when you add a PDF to a note, it automatically names the note with the PDF's title. Furthermore, the way PDFs are displayed within Notes has been enhanced significantly. You can scroll vertically to view each page with ease and choose between three different view sizes – small, medium, and large. The large view allows for comfortable reading of the entire document.

Markup Tools

A significant aspect of this PDF improvement is the markup feature. You can effortlessly mark up the PDF directly within the Notes application. Hovering over text fields allows you to add text, and even better, you can autofill addresses and passwords from your contact and password list. This integration streamlines the annotation process, eliminating the need to switch to the Preview app.

macOS Sonoma User Guide

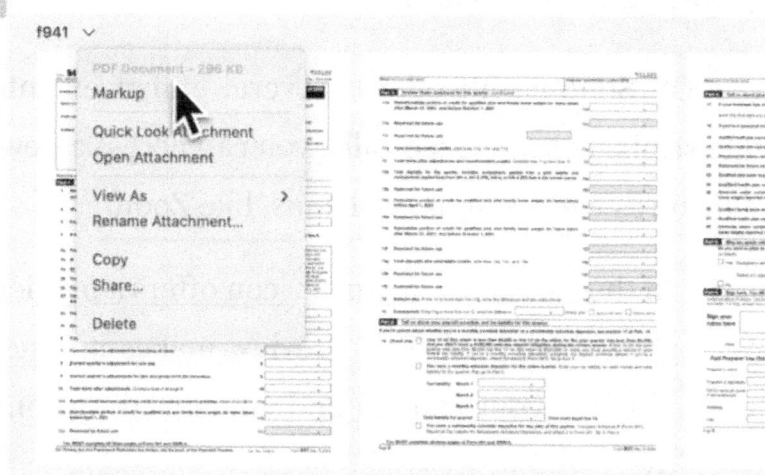

Highlighting and Linking

The markup feature extends to highlighting, allowing you to emphasize specific sections of the document. This feature comes in handy for indicating areas for signatures, initials, or other annotations. Additionally, you can now link to other notes within Mac OS Sonoma by using double greater-than signs, making it easier to navigate between related content.

Enhanced Video Calls

Mac OS Sonoma introduces several enhancements to video calls. During video calls, you can access a new set of features within supported apps, like Zoom.

- In the status bar, a purple icon offers a preview of your video feed. This preview makes it easier to monitor your camera and adjust settings on the fly.
- Within the video feed preview, you can fine-tune your video appearance. You can adjust portrait and studio lights to control your on-screen appearance, helping you look your best during video calls.

AR-Based Reactions

Mac OS Sonoma introduces AR-based reactions for video calls. You can add reactions like thumbs up or hearts that appear as augmented reality elements during your call. These reactions enhance your video call experience.

- A new feature called **Presenter Overlay** allows you to share your screen with a small version of your video feed in the corner, resembling a picture-in-picture effect. This feature is useful for emphasizing points while sharing content. You can choose between small and large overlay styles, depending on your preferences.

- When you hover over the green icon on a window, you can quickly initiate screen sharing for that specific window, streamlining your sharing experience.
- Continuity Camera is enhanced for video calls. Your face is automatically detected and re-centered in the frame, improving the overall video quality without relying on Center Stage.

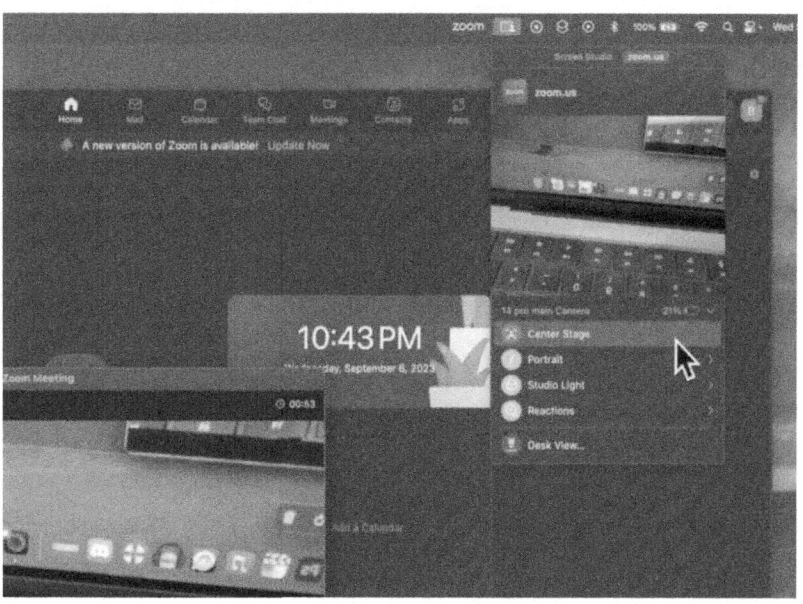

- If you're using another camera, such as an iPhone, you can now select between different camera lenses when using Continuity Camera in video calls. This feature allows you to optimize your video quality.
- Mac OS Sonoma enhances Center Stage by allowing you to choose between the main or ultra-wide camera lens, giving you more control over your video feed.

These video call enhancements make Mac OS Sonoma a valuable tool for remote work and communication, improving your video call experience and flexibility.

Safari and Web Applications

Mac OS Sonoma brings several enhancements to Safari, improving your web browsing experience.

- You can now easily show icons in your favorites on Safari. Right-click or two-finger press on a favorite to reveal the 'Show Icons' option, making it convenient to recognize and access your favorite sites.

Profile Management

Profiles in Safari offer a way to organize your web browsing experience efficiently. You can set up multiple profiles, each with its own set of favorites, preferences, and extensions. This feature is especially useful for differentiating between personal, work, and leisure-related tasks.

- To set up profiles, navigate to Safari settings and select the 'Profiles' section.
- Customize each profile by choosing an icon, main colors, and favorites.

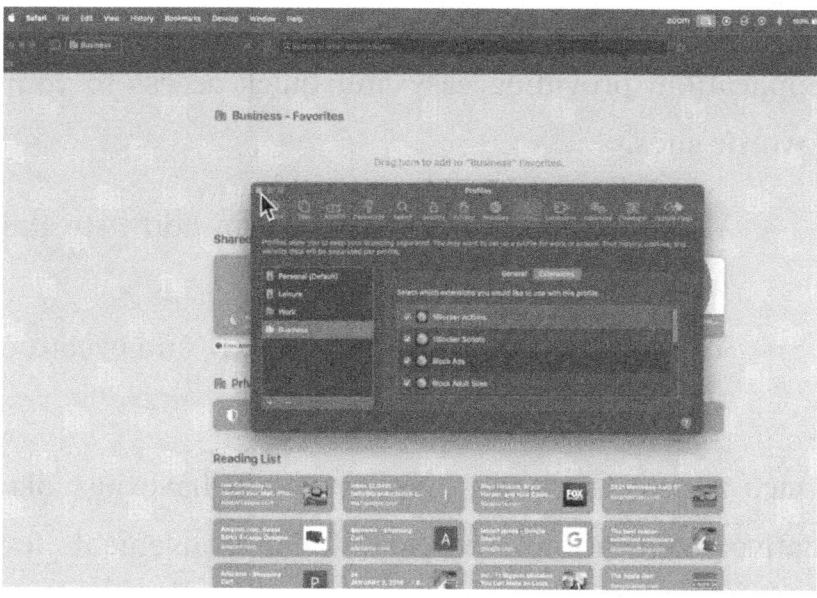

You can specify how new windows and tabs open for each profile, enhancing your control over your browsing experience. Additionally, you can turn extensions on or off on a per-profile basis, ensuring that you have the right set of tools for each task.

- Private windows now feature a lock, which requires Touch ID or a password to access their content. This privacy enhancement provides an extra layer of security for your browsing experience.

Web Applications in the Dock

One of the standout features in Mac OS Sonoma is the ability to add web applications to your dock. This feature allows you to treat any website like a standalone application, providing easy and quick access to your favorite sites.

- When visiting a website, you can add it to the dock by selecting 'Add to Dock.'
- You can customize the name, URL, and even the icon for the web application.

Once added, these web applications behave just like native applications, making them convenient for websites you frequently use.

These Safari and web application enhancements streamline your web browsing experience and offer greater customization, making it easier to access your favorite websites and manage your online activities.

Advanced Privacy Controls

In macOS Sonoma, you'll find advanced privacy controls. In the Privacy section under the Advanced tab, you can enable "Use Advanced tracking and fingerprinting protection." This feature, available in both private and regular browsing, helps prevent websites and companies from precisely tracking you, which is especially important to protect against digital fingerprinting. Be aware that it may remove certain parameters from URLs.

- Safari now offers the option to automatically close tabs after a set period, whether it's after one day, one week, or one month, or you can manage them manually.

Password Sharing with Family

A new feature allows you to share passwords and passkeys with family members. You can customize and name the groups, add members to them, and choose which passwords to share. These groups simplify the management of shared passwords within your family.

Browser Password Manager Extension

Apple's password manager is now available as an extension for third-party browsers like Chrome. This extension provides password autofill and saving capabilities for these browsers, extending the convenience of iCloud Keychain beyond Safari.

- You have increased control over extensions in macOS Sonoma. You can use per-site privacy settings to regulate access for all extensions that require user data, adding a layer of security to your browsing experience.

Game Mode

Gamers will appreciate the new Game Mode, which optimizes system performance for games played in full-screen mode. This mode reduces background task usage and minimizes latency with wireless accessories. DirectX 12 support is also introduced, alongside the ability to disable pointer acceleration for mice, improving precision.

- Screen sharing in macOS Sonoma offers a high-performance mode for responsive remote access over high-bandwidth connections, specifically available for Silicon Macs.
- The Print Center returns in macOS Sonoma, providing a centralized location for print management.

Screen Time Enhancements

Screen Time settings have been reorganized for better clarity and control. They now feature headers for different categories, including activity, limit usage, communication, and restrictions. App and website activity and the new screen distance option for eye strain and myopia prevention are available. A communication safety feature detects sensitive content before it's viewed or sent on a child's device. You can disable app and website activity without turning off Screen Time entirely, and the language has been updated to "Lock Screen Time settings."

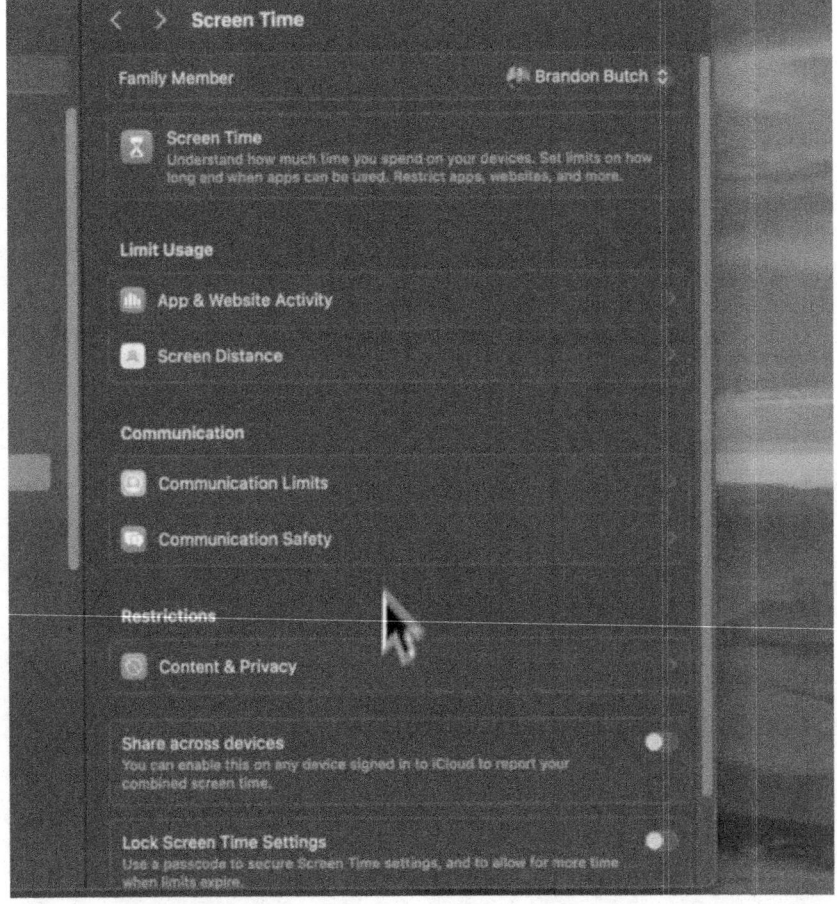

- Throughout macOS Sonoma, you'll find back and forward arrows to facilitate easy navigation between different sections and settings, making it simpler to move between various menu options in the system.

Accessibility and Live Captions

In the realm of Accessibility, macOS Sonoma introduces a significant change to Live Captions. Previously tagged as "beta," Live Captions now stands confidently on its own. Additionally, there's a new glyph icon accompanying VoiceOver under the Motor category. The Speech section has expanded with Live Speech and Personal Voice options. With Live Speech, you can create an AI-generated voice that mimics your own, adding an innovative dimension to accessibility.

- In the Control Center settings, a valuable feature lets you automatically hide and show the menu bar. You can customize it to stay on desktop only, in full-screen mode, or never. Furthermore, in Siri and Spotlight settings, you can now omit the "Hey" before "S" words for more natural interaction, making tasks like voice commands more fluid.
- The Privacy and Security section introduces a new addition: "Sensitive Content Warning." This feature helps detect explicit content, such as nude

photos and videos, before they are displayed on your Mac. This extends beyond the child-focused Screen Time feature and provides a layer of personal security that you can opt to activate.

Location Services and Lockdown Mode

Within **Location Services**, under **System Services**, there's a new option for Alerts and Shortcut Automations, offering more control and versatility. Lockdown Mode has also been revamped with a dedicated page, providing information and guidance before activation.

Stage Manager

Stage Manager now consolidates its customization options into a single, more accessible section, eliminating the need for navigating through a separate window.

Lock Screen and Photos Application

In the Lock Screen settings, you can now decide how and when to display the "Large Clock" and access additional lock screen settings. The Photos application enhances the People tab to include pets, and Visual Lookup becomes even more robust. Visual Lookup can now identify objects like food in your images, offering recipe suggestions. Moreover, you can generate iCloud links for easy sharing of stored photos and videos.

App Improvements

Weather Application

The macOS weather application aligns with its iOS counterpart, offering a comprehensive weather experience. It now includes a wind map and provides information on averages, making it easier to grasp the weather trends at a glance.

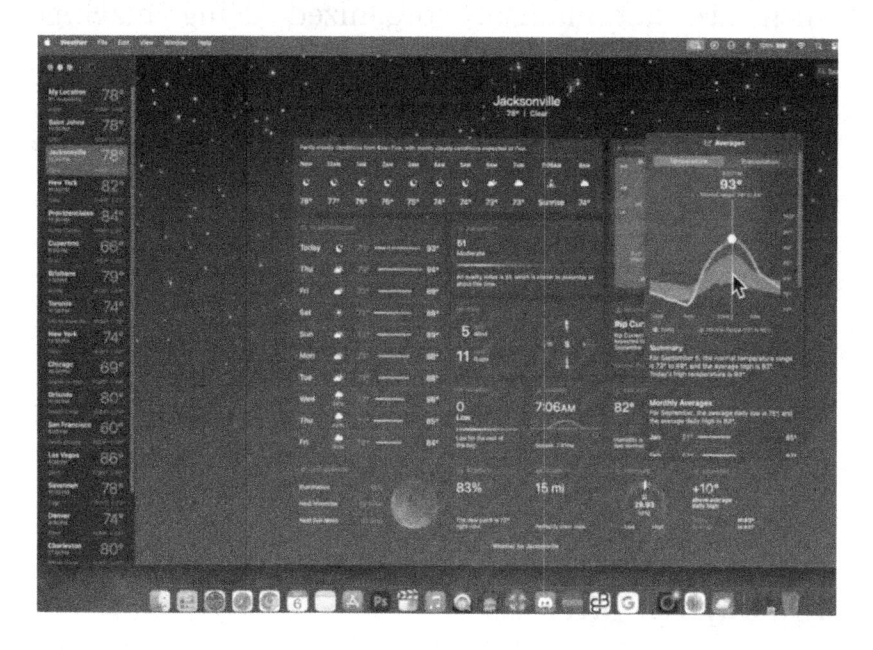

Mail Application

The Mail application introduces a handy feature: it prioritizes travel-related emails as your trip dates approach. You can also add large emojis to your messages. The standout feature is the attachment management, which adds a mail icon to downloaded files in Finder, allowing you to quickly access and reply to the corresponding email.

Reminders Application

The Reminders application now supports grocery lists, which are automatically organized using machine learning. You can switch to a column view for a more spacious layout, and items are auto-categorized, simplifying list management.

Notes Application

In the Notes application, a new paragraph style called "Monospaced" has been introduced, providing an alternative text style. You can also finish a note in Pages directly from the share sheet.

Messages Application

The Messages application on macOS Sonoma offers new search filters, which make it easier to find specific content in conversations. Stickers have also made their way to the desktop, allowing for expressive and fun communication. Stickers can be used in messages, the Freeform application, and various other contexts.

Find My Application

The Find My application now empowers users to share an AirTag or Find My accessory with up to five people, simplifying collaborative tracking. The 'Share This Item' section allows you to initiate and manage shared access effortlessly.

Home Application

In the Home application, Mac users will appreciate the addition of activity history, providing a comprehensive overview of your HomeKit-enabled devices' past interactions. This is a valuable feature for keeping track of your smart home's operations and security.

Enhanced Video Encoding

For video editing enthusiasts, macOS Sonoma brings a boost in video encoding speed, especially for those using an M1 Ultra or M2 Ultra machine. This performance improvement extends to popular video editing applications like Final Cut Pro, Compressor, and various third-party video editing tools, enhancing productivity and efficiency in the content creation process.

Minor UI Tweaks

For the eagle-eyed users who appreciate the finer details, macOS Sonoma introduces subtle changes in the user interface. The Spotlight search bar and the dock feature more rounded edges, offering a sleek and modern look. Even the app icons have been gently refined, exhibiting a subtle yet pleasing departure from the previous Ventura design. These nuanced adjustments contribute to a more polished and cohesive visual experience across the operating system.

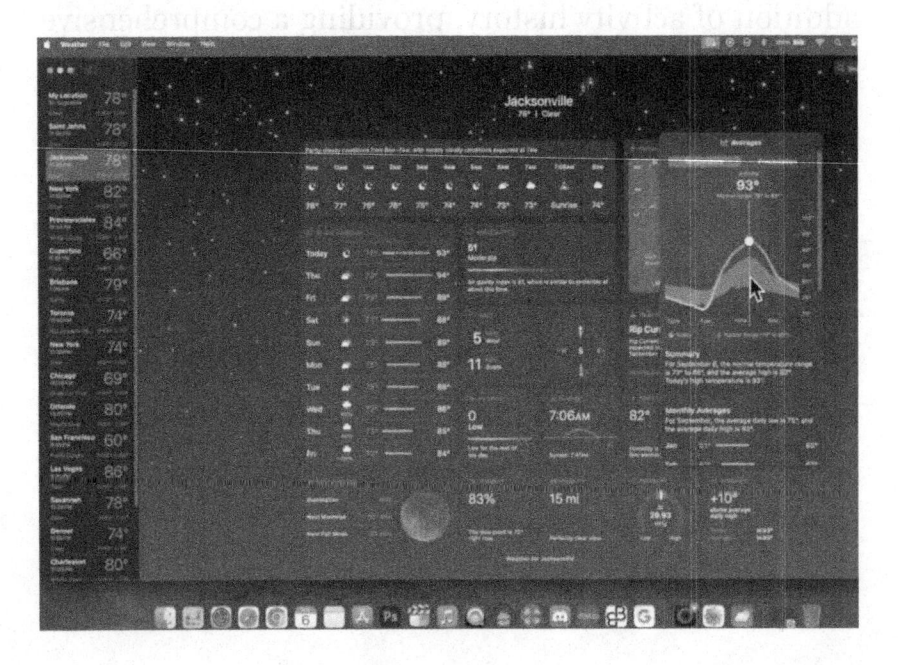

These features and improvements in macOS Sonoma enhance privacy, security, gaming performance, and overall usability. The reorganized Screen Time settings and navigation enhancements further streamline the user experience in the operating system.

Chapter 2: Mac Basics for Beginners

In this chapter, I will share with you the essentials of the Mac operating system. If you're transitioning from a Windows computer, you'll notice that the Control key on Windows corresponds to the Command key on a Mac. For instance, in Windows, you'd use Control + C to copy, while on a Mac, you'd use Command + C for the same action. The same goes for pasting; use Command + V instead.

Over time, you'll find that using Control instead of Command can feel less ergonomic. Another unique feature of the Mac is its drag-and-drop-oriented system.

You can effortlessly move files, text, images, and more throughout the operating system.

To delete something, simply drag it to the trash can. You can also eject a disk by dragging it to the trash. This same method works for deleting files, apps, or colors from your palette.

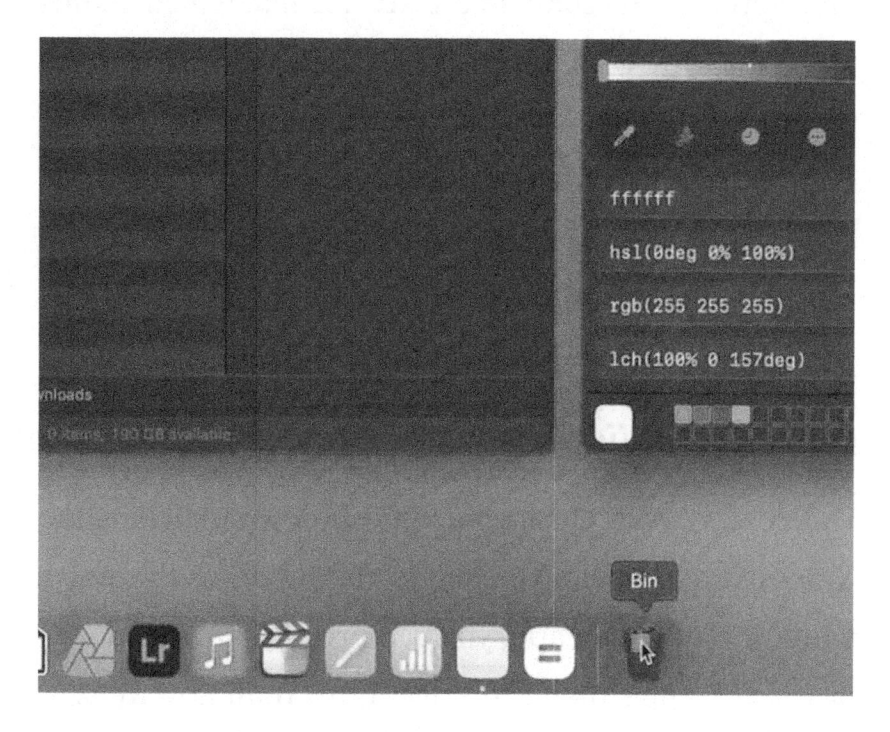

On a Mac, you won't find the familiar start menu, control panel, or add/remove programs like on Windows. If you no longer need something, just put it in the trash. And if you haven't emptied the trash, you can restore items easily.

- Out of the box, the right-click function is disabled on a Mac. You can enable it in settings, allowing you to right-click by pressing the Control key and clicking with the cursor.

Software and Applications

Mac applications come in a DMG format, which stands for Mac OS X Disk Image file. When you download a program for your Mac, it's typically in DMG format. Think of a DMG file as inserting a CD with software. When you open a DMG file, it behaves as if you've inserted a physical disk into your computer. When you're done with it, just eject the disk.

Quitting Applications

Unlike Windows, closing an app window by clicking the X doesn't quit the app on a Mac; it only closes the active window. To quit an app, you can press **Command + Q** or use the app's menu to select quit. If an app freezes, you can force quit it from the Apple menu.

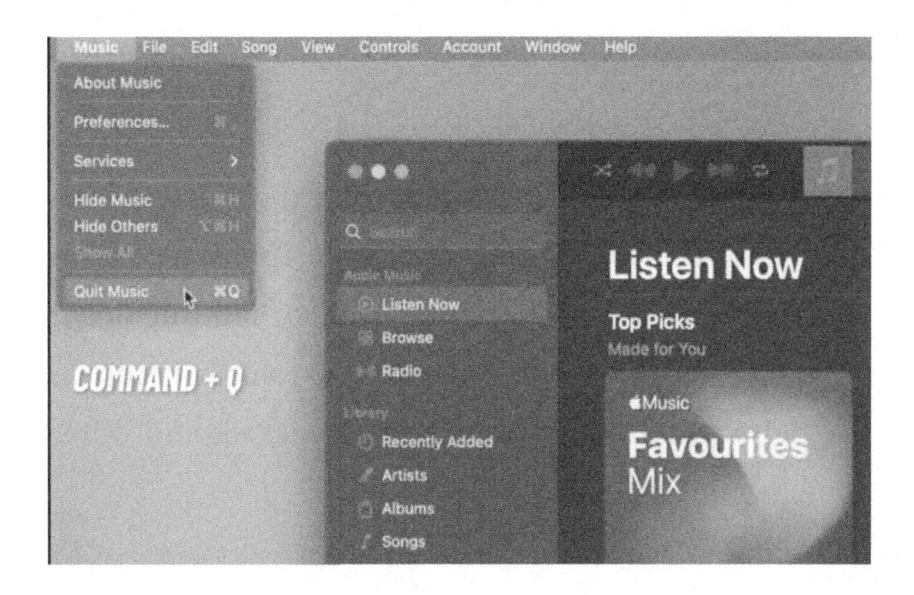

No "Cut," Only "Copy"

On the Mac, there's no "Cut" function, just "Copy." Given its drag-and-drop nature, moving items is as simple as dragging and dropping them.

Sleep Mode vs. Shutdown

Unlike Windows, you don't need to turn off your Mac computer regularly. You can put it to sleep and resume where you left off. This won't slow down your Mac.

Overview of Mac Interface

When you power up your Mac, you'll see the desktop, similar to Windows. You can organize files and folders on the desktop, just like any other computer. You can even have multiple desktops, making it easier to manage different applications.

At the top of the screen, you'll find the menu bar, which changes depending on the active app. The Apple menu on the left holds essential functions like shutting down or accessing System Preferences. The toolbar items on the right remain consistent, with the clock and other app-specific elements.

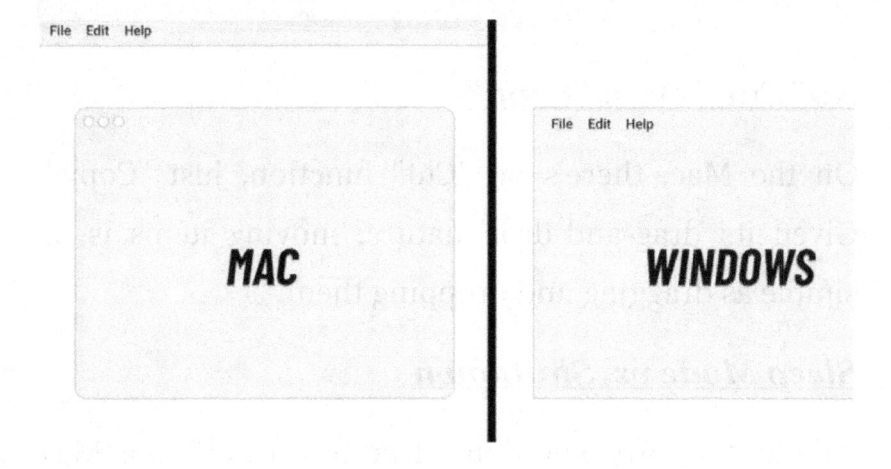

The **Dock**, located at the bottom of the screen, serves as a hub for your active apps and open windows. You can customize it to match your workflow and easily access frequently used apps. When you minimize a window, it slides into the Dock, ready to be reopened.

Apps running in the background typically have a small dot beneath their icon in the Dock, indicating that they're active. If there's no dot, the app isn't running. You can also add quick access to folders like Downloads next to the trash can. The Dock is highly customizable, so you can adapt it to your needs, whether that means making it fuller, larger, minimal, or even invisible.

Unlike the Windows operating system, where the control buttons for windows are on the right side, Mac OS has them on the left. These buttons resemble a traffic light, with red for close, yellow for minimize, and green for expand. Each app or window on Mac has these control buttons on the left.

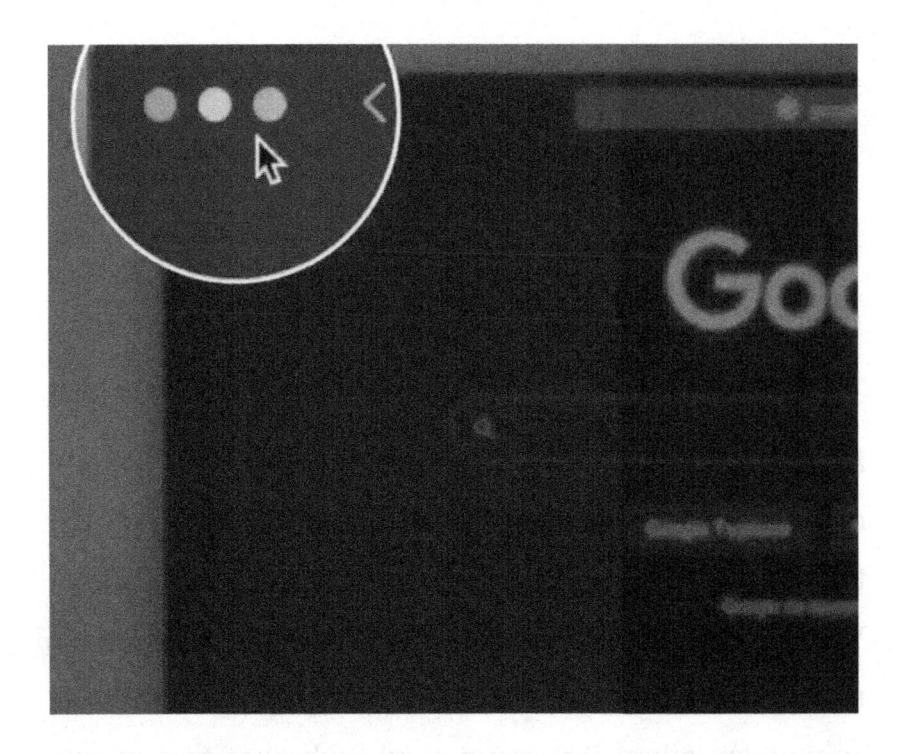

All your applications live in the Applications folder. While you can start them from there, a more convenient option is to use the Launchpad, which you can access from the dock. It functions much like an iPhone, with a grid of app icons that you can rearrange and organize into folders for easy access.

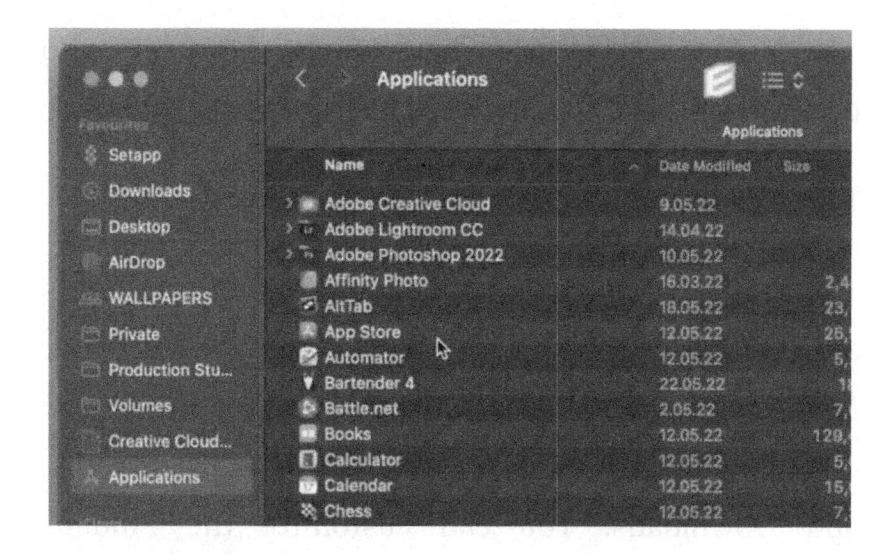

System Settings

Most of your macOS settings can be found in the Apple menu under System Preferences. Here, you can customize various aspects, from changing your desktop wallpaper to setting up keyboard input methods and accessibility options, like enabling the right-click on your mouse.

Spotlight Search

Spotlight is your go-to global system search. You can find files, photos, or even look up dictionary explanations with it. To activate Spotlight, you can either click the magnifying glass or use the shortcut **CMD+Space**, which is a quick and efficient way to search for and launch applications. You can also perform simple calculations right from Spotlight.

The Finder

The Finder is equivalent to Windows Explorer and is crucial for accessing all your files. When you start your Mac, the desktop is part of the Finder, and it contains default folders like Desktop, Music, Photos, Documents, and Downloads. You can customize the Finder's interface to suit your preferences. Creating folders is simple – just right-click in an empty space to create one, and to rename it, click on it or use the right-click menu for more options.

Finder also provides a convenient feature to archive files. Select a group of files, right-click, and choose "Archive" to quickly send an archive to someone. And when it comes to deleting items on a Mac, including apps from the Applications folder, it's as easy as dragging them to the trash can.

File Preview

One of the most useful features on Mac is the ability to preview files. Whether it's a video or a photo, simply select a file and press the spacebar to preview it. If you have multiple images, you can use the arrow keys to move around and preview them all.

Preview is a versatile default app that can open various file types, including documents, images, and PDF files. Safari is the default browser on Mac, but you can install other browsers like Chrome if you prefer. The App Store on macOS is similar to the one on the iPhone, offering a wide range of applications. Every app from the App Store is considered secure and tested.

Installing Apps

If you install an app that's not in the App Store, you'll typically download a DMG file. To install such apps, open the DMG file, and you'll often see an arrow or shortcut to drag the app into your computer's Applications folder. Think of it as moving a song from a CD to your hard drive. Once the app is in the

Applications folder, you can eject and delete the DMG if necessary.

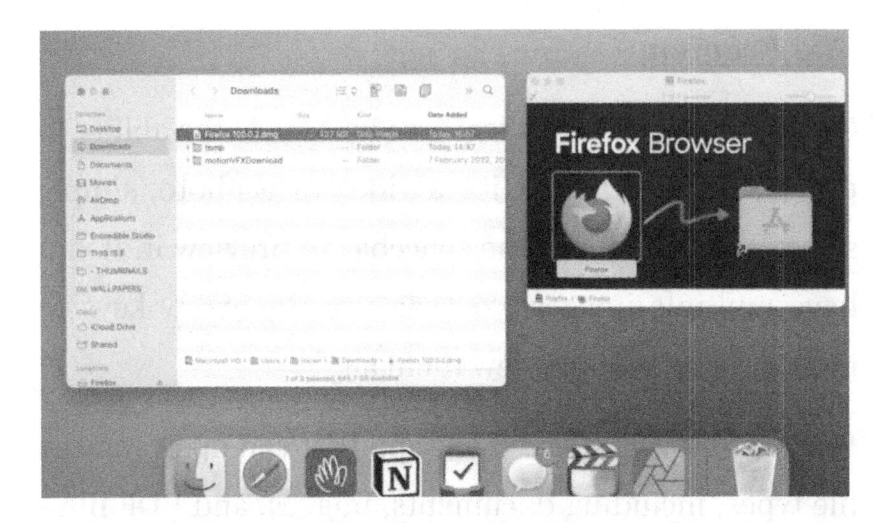

Deleting apps from the App Store is straightforward. Open the Launchpad and hold down an app until they start jiggling. Apps from the App Store can be deleted by pressing the "X" icon.

iCloud

iCloud is an integral part of macOS, offering cloud-based storage solutions. It allows you to sync data across your Apple devices and provides iCloud Drive, an online hard drive. When you set up your Mac, you'll be asked to create or sign in to an iCloud account. This feature is handy for accessing your data from anywhere.

Useful Shortcuts

Here are some essential keyboard shortcuts to help you navigate your Mac more efficiently:

- Command+Q: Quits an app
- Command+C: Copies
- Command+V: Pastes
- Command+H: Hides an app or a window
- Command+Space: Activates Spotlight
- Command+Tab: Switches between active apps
- Control+Space: Changes language input
- Command+I: Opens additional file info
- Command+F: Searches for content
- Command+/-: Zooms in and out
- Option, Command, and Esc: Opens the Force Quit Menu for closing unresponsive apps.
- Command + L: Selects the full URL of the current website for quick copying.
- Option + Command + H: Hides all open windows, leaving only the active app visible.
- Control + Command + Space: Access emojis.
- Shift + Command + 5: Opens the Screen Recording Menu for recording and screenshots, allowing customization of screenshot folders.

- Command + [Left or Right Bracket]: Navigate backward and forward in Finder, useful for file organization.
- Control + Command + Q: Quickly locks the screen, handy for office scenarios.
- Command + Comma: Opens the settings window of the currently active app.

The Option key unlocks hidden features, like toggling Do Not Disturb by tapping on the clock in the Apple Menu.

Zooming Systemwide

- Open System Settings.
- Go to Accessibility.
- Under Vision, select Zoom.
- Enable "Use scroll gesture with modifier key" and choose the Control button, for example.
- Once enabled, hold Control and scroll in/out to zoom to the mouse pointer location.

Screenshot Capture

- Press **Command + Shift + 3** to capture the entire screen.

- The screenshot appears briefly on the screen and saves to your desktop or chosen location.
- To capture a specific element, press **Command + Shift + 4** to turn the cursor into a crosshair icon.
- Drag to select the area, and the screenshot displays dimensions in pixels.

This method is perfect for quick graphic tasks.

Showcasing Websites and Apps

- To present a website or app feature:
- Open the webpage or app.
- Press Command + Shift + 4.
- Press the space bar to capture windows.

This feature also includes a built-in shadow effect.

Text Formatting Removal

- Avoid pasting unwanted formatting by using Command + Option + Shift + V to paste as plain text.

File Renaming

- Select a file and press Return to quickly rename it.

- MacOS often excludes the file extension from the selection.
- To batch rename files, select them and right-click, then choose the "Rename" option.

Apple Watch Integration

Apple Watch can automatically unlock your Mac.

- Enable this feature in System Settings, Touch ID and Password, by selecting the Watch using the same Apple ID as your Mac.

Save time by avoiding the need to type a lengthy password.

Quick App Quitting

- Use Command + Tab to move between active apps.
- To quickly quit an app, while Command-tabbing, press Command + Q.

Handy for decluttering your workspace after completing tasks.

Image Size Conversion

- In Finder, select the images you want to convert.

- Right-click to open the Quick Actions menu and choose "Convert Image."
- Change image formats and even select a smaller size with MacOS estimating the new file sizes.

Original files are not replaced; copies are created.

Chapter 3: A Windows User's Guide to Mac Basics

Welcome to this beginner's tutorial for using macOS. I'll frame things from the perspective of a Windows user to help those who are new to Mac understand the differences between the two operating systems.

This tutorial should be helpful even if you've never used a computer before. I'll be going into quite a bit of detail, covering all the main features of macOS.

Let's begin by exploring a crucial area of macOS – the Apple menu located at the top left corner. Clicking on it reveals a range of core functions, somewhat similar to the Start menu in Windows.

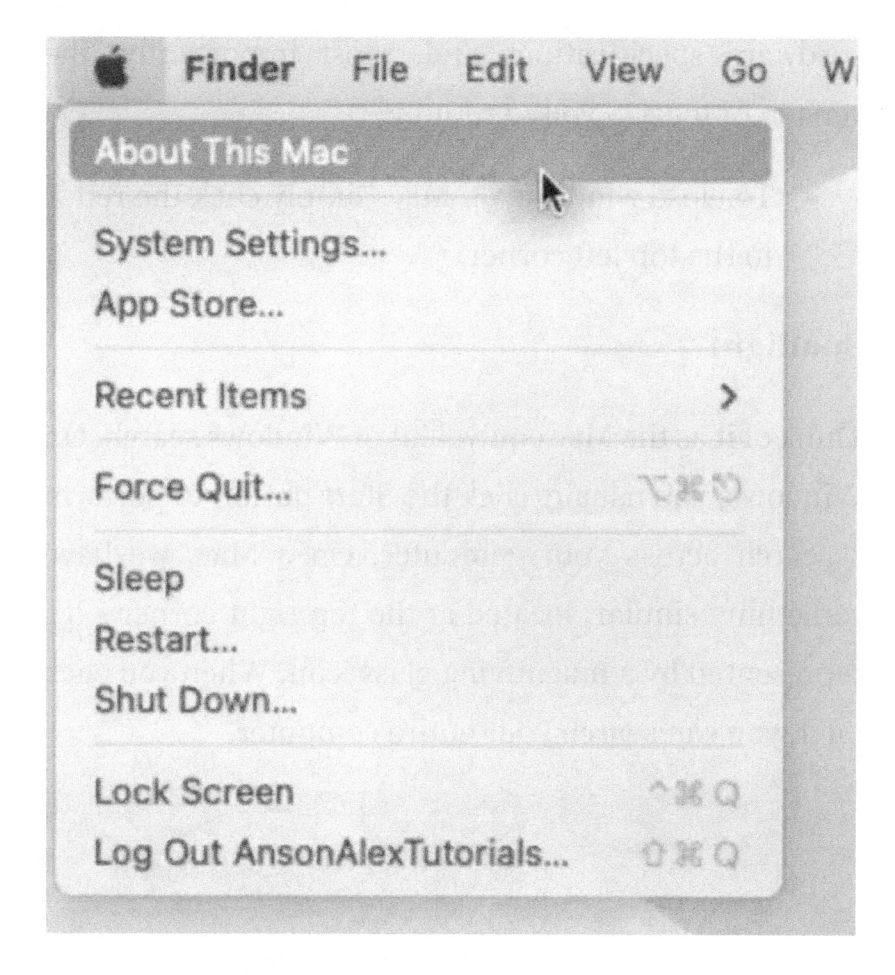

```
                    Finder    File    Edit    View    Go    W
┌─────────────────────────────────────────────┐
│ About This Mac                              │
│                                             │
│ System Settings...                          │
│ App Store...                                │
│                                             │
│ Recent Items                              > │
│                                             │
│ Force Quit...                        ⌥⌘⎋   │
│                                             │
│ Sleep                                       │
│ Restart...                                  │
│ Shut Down...                                │
│                                             │
│ Lock Screen                          ⌃⌘Q   │
│ Log Out AnsonAlexTutorials...        ⇧⌘Q   │
└─────────────────────────────────────────────┘
```

Here, you'll find options to:

- Restart your computer.
- Shut it down.
- Put it to sleep.

Access system settings (which is akin to the Control Panel on Windows). "About This Mac" feature provides detailed information about your Mac, including hardware specifications and, most importantly, the version of macOS you're running.

- To close windows on Mac, simply click the red X in the top left corner.

Spotlight

Think of it as the Mac equivalent of Windows search. On Windows, you usually click the Start button to perform a search across your computer. On a Mac, we have something similar, located at the top right corner - it's represented by a magnifying glass icon. When you click on it, you can search your entire computer.

- The keyboard shortcuts to open Spotlight is **Command + Spacebar**.

Spotlight search allows you to search for files, folders, documents, applications, movies, music, or anything else on your Mac.

If you can't find what you're looking for in Spotlight, you can scroll to the bottom of the results and select "search in Finder" to search for the file on your computer.

At the bottom of your screen, there's a toolbar with various applications. Let's briefly go through some of them:

- Finder: This is like Windows Explorer and is essential for managing your files and folders.
- Launchpad: It provides quick access to your applications.
- Safari: Apple's web browser.
- iMessage: Use it to send messages from your Mac.
- Mail: An email application, although some prefer using webmail.
- Maps: Apple Maps for navigation.
- Photos: Manage your photos and videos.
- FaceTime: Video calls and messaging.
- Calendar: Apple's calendar system.

- Contacts: Access your contacts.
- Reminders: Create to-do lists.
- Notes: Similar to digital sticky notes.
- Apple TV, Apple Music, and Apple News: For entertainment and news.
- Keynote, Numbers, and Pages: Apple's word processing applications, equivalent to Microsoft Office.
- App Store: Where you can download apps and software.
- System settings: Manage your Mac's settings.

Downloads folder

When you download a file from the Internet, it typically goes into this folder.

- You can reach your Downloads folder through Finder, or you can simply click on "Downloads" in the toolbar to open it.

A noteworthy point about Macs is the similarity they share with Windows in terms of computing. One fundamental concept is the right-click. If you're ever in doubt, you can usually right-click to access options. For example, if you want to empty your trash, just right-click, and you'll find the option to empty the trash. You can right-click on your desktop to create folders, similar to how you would on a Windows desktop.

The desktop on Mac functions like a workspace. You can place files and folders on it, and it's a great place to organize your work. Additionally, you can change your desktop wallpaper for a personalized touch. Remember, when in doubt, right-click.

Settings

- Navigate to the system settings, which are known as "System Preferences."

You can access various settings like Wi-Fi, Bluetooth devices, and notification management. If certain apps are bothering you with notifications, you can disable them here. Additionally, you can adjust sound settings, customize your display options, and keep an eye on your screen time.

The "General" section is packed with features. Here, you can check for software updates, monitor your storage usage, and set up Airdrop for quick file sharing between your iPhone and Mac. Managing startup items is simpler on Mac than it used to be on Windows. You can control which applications start when you log in and enable or disable them as needed.

Within the "Language & Region" section, you can customize your language, region, date, and time settings. If you're using Time Machine for backups, you can manage those settings here. In the "Appearance" section, you can adjust how your Mac's interface looks, including themes and lighting adjustments.

In the "Accessibility" section, you'll find options for customizing your Mac to meet your specific needs. These accessibility features can enhance your user experience.

These are just a few of the system settings and features you can explore to personalize and optimize your Mac. Don't hesitate to dive into them and make your Mac experience truly your own.

Privacy and security options is crucial for managing location services and app permissions. You can review which apps are requesting access to your location. It's a good idea to explore these settings on your own time to get a better understanding of your computer's capabilities.

Additionally, you can change your default web browser if you prefer using something other than Safari. You can also customize your display settings, including screen resolution.

- **Tip**: If you right-click on one of the resolution squares, you can select "Show List" to view a list of resolutions, making it easier to choose the one that suits your needs.

Finder

- To access Finder, go to the dock at the bottom and click on the Finder icon. This will open a window that's akin to Windows Explorer, where you can navigate your computer's file system.

Within Finder, you'll find a "Recent" section that displays any documents you've worked on recently. On the left side, you have access to various locations, such as the Applications folder, which contains a variety of applications. You can sort the view by name or other criteria and change the way you view the content using the view options at the top.

You have four main view options:

- <u>Icon View</u>: This is the default view for applications, displaying icons.
- <u>List View</u>: Suitable for folders with files and subfolders, providing a detailed list.
- <u>Hierarchy View</u>: Great for exploring nested folders, showing a folder's content in a tree-like structure.
- <u>Gallery View</u>: Ideal for browsing images and videos.

Each view has its use, and you can switch between them depending on your needs. For instance, List View is handy for organized folder structures, while Gallery View is excellent for media files.

File Previews

When viewing files on your computer, especially images, you can easily preview them.

- Just click on an image or application.
- Then, press the spacebar, no other key is needed.
- If it's an image or video, a preview will pop up, and videos will play.
- For applications, you'll see information like version, size, and modification date.

- You can also share or open the application from this preview.

Organizing Files on Desktop

- To access applications, navigate to the applications folder.
- For your desktop, it's like a virtual view of your physical desktop.
- You can create folders to organize your desktop.
- Right-click on the desktop in Finder, select "New Folder," and name it.

Desktop and Folders

- The folder you create in Finder appears on your desktop.
- You can manage files on the desktop through Finder.
- On Windows, you can do similar operations.
- The Documents folder is a place to store documents. You can create subfolders within it for better organization.

Downloads Folder

- By default, downloads from web browsers go to the Downloads folder. If you can't find downloaded files, check here.

iCloud Drive and Boot Camp

- iCloud Drive stores files in iCloud for backup and remote access.
- Boot Camp allows running Windows on Mac, accessible through Applications > Utilities.

Customizing Finder

In Finder, you have various menu options.

- Click "Finder" and choose "Settings" to customize Finder.
- Check "Hard Disks" to see hard drives on the desktop.
- Double-clicking your hard drive takes you to the root of your computer.

Generally, you'll explore the Users folder, containing your Home folder.

- In your Home folder, you'll find subfolders like Desktop, Documents, Downloads, Movies, Music, and Pictures. These are just folders and can be customized.

- You can drag frequently used folders to the left sidebar in Finder for quick access.
- You can add "Connected Servers" to the sidebar. This helps if you remotely connect to servers.
- You can change what the new Finder window shows, such as Recents, your hard drive, Documents, or Desktop.

Customizing Finder

You can personalize Finder settings to suit your preferences.

- In the "Sidebar" section, you can add folders like Music and Pictures to the sidebar for quick access.
- Under "Advanced," you can enable "Show all file name extensions" to see file types more clearly.
- You can set the trash to empty automatically after 30 days if desired.

There are other options available in Finder settings.

Working with Multiple Finder Windows

- You can open multiple Finder windows to move files more easily.

- For instance, you can drag files between different locations.
- Keyboard shortcuts for copy and paste are similar to Windows (Command + C, Command + V).

Keyboard Shortcuts on Mac

Mac uses Command instead of Control for most keyboard shortcuts.

- For example, Command + C to copy and Command + V to paste.

File Management in Finder

- To delete files, right-click and select "Move to Trash."
- Empty the trash by right-clicking the trash icon in the dock and choosing "Empty Trash."
- You can also restore items from the trash by selecting "Put Back."

View Options in Finder

- In the "View" menu, you can customize how files and folders are displayed in Finder.
- You can change icon sizes, grid spacing, and text size for better visibility.

- You can also sort files and folders from this menu.
- Additionally, there is an option to show view options.

Managing Windows

- The red X button in the window's upper-left corner closes the window but doesn't quit the application.
- To quit an application, use the application's menu (e.g., Safari > Quit Safari) or press Command + Q.
- The yellow button minimizes the window to the dock. You can also use Command + M as a keyboard shortcut to minimize.
- The green button can maximize the window to full screen or have other functions like tiling. Mouse over the green button to access these options.

Using Safari

- Open Safari from the dock by clicking it once.
- The red X closes the Safari window but doesn't quit the application. To quit Safari, use the Safari menu or Command + Q.

- The yellow button minimizes the Safari window to the dock. You can also use Command + M for this.
- The green button can have different functions, such as tiling and screen placement. Mouse over it to access these options.

Safari functions similarly to other web browsers like Google Chrome and Firefox.

- To get started, you can enter a website or perform a search in the address bar.
- Use the back and forward buttons to navigate web pages.
- The share button is available for sharing web pages.
- You can open a new tab by clicking the plus icon or by using the keyboard shortcut Command + T.

Safari Menus

- You can access Safari settings by clicking the Safari menu, which is a common approach for many applications.
- In settings, you can customize various options, such as startup preferences, homepage selection, autofill, and search engine choice.

Bookmarks in Safari

- To add a new bookmark, go to the bookmarks menu and select "Add Bookmark." Choose the location to save it.
- Access your bookmarks by clicking on "Show Bookmarks" in the bookmarks menu, which will appear on the left side of the screen.
- To hide the bookmarks, click "Hide Bookmarks" in the bookmarks menu.

Installing Applications on Mac

When installing an application on Mac, the installation file is typically a .dmg file.

- Double-click the .dmg file, which will usually open a window with the application's icon.
- To install the application, drag and drop the icon into your Applications folder. You may need to provide your administrator password.

Many Mac applications do not require a traditional installation process and can be used immediately.

Installing Google Chrome

- You can download Google Chrome from the official website (e.g., chrome.google.com).
- After downloading, the file will appear in your Downloads folder.
- To install, double-click the .dmg file, then drag and drop the Chrome icon into your Applications folder.
- You can launch Google Chrome from Spotlight (Command + Spacebar) or by navigating to your Applications folder and double-clicking it.

Resizing Windows

- To resize windows on Mac, you can drag from a corner or edge to make them larger or smaller.

Managing Dock

In macOS, you can manage the applications in your Dock.

- To keep an application in the Dock even when it's not running, right-click its icon in the Dock, go to Options, and select "Keep in Dock."
- To remove an app from the Dock, click and drag its icon off the Dock, and it will disappear.

- You can personalize your Dock by keeping only the applications you frequently use.

Closing Applications

Closing an application window on Mac doesn't necessarily quit the application itself.

- To close a window, click the red X button.
- To quit an application completely, use the application's menu (e.g., Chrome > Quit Chrome) or press Command + Q.

Ejecting Drives

If you have a removable drive (e.g., a flash drive) connected to your Mac, you can safely eject it.

- Right-click the drive on your desktop and select "Eject [Drive Name]" to remove it.

This ensures that your drive is disconnected safely without data loss.

Quickly Managing WiFi

- You can manage your WiFi connection from the top-right corner of the screen.
- Click on the WiFi symbol to select and switch between available networks.

Patrick B. Hurtado

Customizing your Dock with the applications you use often is a good place to start. Start exploring and experimenting to become more comfortable with macOS.

Chapter 4: Stage Manager and Mission Control

In this chapter, we're going to explore the wonderful world of Stage Manager and Mission Control, two powerful tools that can help you navigate the chaos of open windows on your Mac. If you're anything like me, you probably find yourself buried under a mountain of windows, including your email, web browser, music player, and more. It's time to regain control and boost your productivity. Let's dive right in.

Introducing Stage Manager

First, let's set the stage with a typical work scenario. Imagine having Safari, Apple Photos, Pages, Music, and Calendar all open at once. The result? A cluttered mess of overlapping windows. It's not only frustrating but also counterproductive. This is where Stage Manager comes to the rescue.

- Open Safari, Apple Photos, Pages, Music, and Calendar.
- Watch as the windows stack on top of each other.

- Try minimizing a window to the dock by clicking the top left corner.

To utilize Stage Manager, you need to enable it first.

- Click on the Apple logo in the top left.
- Access System Preferences.

If you're having trouble finding it in the new operating system, use the search in the top left.

- Type "Stage" in the search bar.
- Under Desktop and Dock, you'll find Stage Manager.
- Toggle it on.

Now, observe how all your open windows move out of the way, leaving you focused on the primary task at hand (System Settings). You can quickly switch between apps by hovering over icons on the left-hand side.

Customizing Stage Manager

Stage Manager offers some customization options to enhance your experience.

- To show recent applications, move your cursor to the left-hand side.

- To hide or show items on your desktop, toggle the option as per your preference.
- To control how windows from an application are displayed, choose between "all at once" or "one at a time."
- The "one at a time" option lets you cycle through multiple windows without overlapping them.
- Hold down Shift and click to bring all the windows forward.

If you prefer easy access to Stage Manager, you can add it to your menu bar.

- Go to System Preferences.
- Select Control Center.
- Find Stage Manager.
- Choose "show in menu bar" for one-click access.

Another quick way to toggle Stage Manager on and off is by holding down the Option key and clicking the icon in the menu bar. It's all about making things as efficient as possible.

With Stage Manager, you can regain control of your desktop and focus on one task at a time. Whether you prefer to view all your windows at once or cycle through them, Stage Manager empowers you to multitask like a pro. Say goodbye to window clutter and hello to enhanced productivity.

Mission Control

Imagine a screen cluttered with overlapping windows, making it frustrating to find what you need. Mission Control comes to the rescue.

- Turn off Stage Manager by going to the top right.

Now, your windows are stacked up.

- To activate Mission Control, swipe up on your trackpad with three fingers. This action provides a bird's eye view of all open applications, allowing you to click on the one you want, eliminating the need to shuffle windows around.

Mission Control has another trick up its sleeve - the ability to create multiple virtual desktops.

- By moving your cursor to the top of the screen, you'll see options for "Desktop 1" and "Desktop 2."
- Swipe up with three fingers to see them in action.
- On the far right, you can add more virtual desktops to organize your work efficiently.

Imagine these virtual desktops as additional screens, each dedicated to specific tasks. You can drag applications to the desktops where they belong.

- For example, assign Safari to desktop 3, Music to desktop 5, and Calendar to a new desktop.
- Use three fingers up to switch between these virtual desktops seamlessly.
- Swipe left with three fingers to navigate to the next desktop.

This way, your windows won't overlap, and you can truly focus on one task at a time.

Customizing Desktops

You can personalize your virtual desktops even further by setting different wallpapers for each.

- Select a desktop, go to "Set Wallpaper," and choose a background image.

Now, visually differentiate between your virtual desktops.

Keyboard Shortcuts for Quick Access

For those who prefer a mouse or want to streamline your actions further, you can assign keyboard shortcuts.

- Open System Preferences.
- Navigate to Keyboard Shortcuts.
- Explore the available shortcuts for Mission Control and Stage Manager.
- Personalize your shortcuts to your liking for a seamless experience.

Mastering Your Trackpad

The trackpad on your laptop is a powerful tool that can surpass the capabilities of a standard mouse. Get comfortable with your trackpad to enhance your Mac experience.

- Learn the basics of the trackpad's gestures, including right-clicking or secondary clicking.
- Explore the options in System Preferences > Trackpad to customize its behavior.
- Familiarize yourself with gestures like three-finger swipes to navigate Mission Control.

It might take some time to adjust, but with practice, you'll discover the convenience of using the trackpad.

Stage Manager and Mission Control are just two of the many tools available on your Mac to enhance multitasking. Whether you prefer the simplicity of the trackpad or the precision of a mouse, you have the power to customize your experience to suit your needs. Give it a try, and you might find that these features significantly improve your productivity on your Mac.

Chapter 5: Mastering macOS: Essential Mac Getting Started Tips

In this chapter, I will walk you through over 30 Mac getting started tips. This can be handy if you purchased a brand-new Mac or if you've just reinstalled macOS. Even if you're a seasoned Mac user, chances are there will probably be a few of these tips in here that are going to be helpful for you as well.

Adjust Tracking Speed

- Open **System Preferences**.
- Navigate to **Trackpad**.
- Locate the tracking speed slider set at level four by default.
- Drag the slider almost all the way to the right, second to the last position, for faster tracking speed.

Enable Tap to Click

- In **System Preferences**, find the Trackpad section.

- By default, tap to click is disabled.
- Enable it to click by just tapping on the trackpad.

Enable Three-Finger Drag

- Go to **System Preferences**.
- Find **Accessibility**.
- Scroll down to **Pointer Control**.
- Click on **Trackpad Options**.
- Enable Dragging and select Three-Finger Drag from the drop-down box.
- Click OK.

Now, you can drag windows or items without physically clicking.

Adjust Mouse Tracking Speed

- Open System Preferences.
- Navigate to Mouse.
- Adjust the tracking speed to your preference for more efficient mouse movement.

Enable Secondary Click (Right-Click) for Magic Mouse

- In System Preferences > Mouse, enable secondary click functionality.

This allows you to right-click by clicking the right side of your Magic Mouse.

Configure Swipe Between Pages for Magic Mouse

- Open System Preferences > Mouse.
- Click on More Gestures.
- Enable Swipe Between Pages.
- Use swipe gestures to navigate back and forth in applications like Safari.

Set Up Apple Watch Unlock

- Open System Preferences.
- Navigate to Security & Privacy.
- Click on "Use your Apple Watch to unlock apps and your Mac."
- Configure and approve the use of your Apple Watch to unlock your Mac and specific apps.

You can also use the Apple Watch to unlock your Mac at the lock screen.

Setting Up Hot Corners

- Go to System Preferences.
- Click on Mission Control.
- In the bottom left-hand corner, click on Hot Corners.

Now, configure each of the four corners:

Bottom Left-Hand Corner: Show Desktop

- Select 'Desktop' in this corner.

Upper Left-Hand Corner: Launchpad

- Assign 'Launchpad' to this corner.

Upper Right-Hand Corner: Mission Control

- Choose 'Mission Control' for this corner.

Bottom Right-Hand Corner: Put Display to Sleep

- Assign 'Put Display to Sleep' to this corner.

Click OK to save your settings.

Using Hot Corners

- To show the desktop, move your cursor to the bottom left-hand corner.

- To open Launchpad, move your cursor to the upper left-hand corner.
- To access Mission Control, move your cursor to the upper right-hand corner.
- To put the display to sleep, move your cursor to the bottom right-hand corner.

Feel free to configure your hot corners to your preference.

Enabling Keyboard Navigation

- Go to System Preferences.
- Click on Keyboard.
- Select the Shortcuts tab.
- Check the box that says 'Use keyboard navigation to move focus between controls'.

This will enhance keyboard navigation capabilities within macOS, providing better control and efficiency.

Customizing Your Computer Name

- To update your computer name, press Return after renaming it in System Preferences.

- Choose a more descriptive name, which is particularly useful if you have multiple Macs on the same network.

Quick Access to Sound Settings

- Open Control Center.
- Drag the Sound module to the menu bar.
- Holding option while clicking the Sound icon allows you to access both input and output settings conveniently.

This streamlines access to sound controls with fewer clicks.

Removing Spotlight from the Menu Bar

- Hold the Command key on your keyboard.
- Click and drag the Spotlight icon from the menu bar and release to remove it.

This is especially useful if you prefer to use keyboard shortcuts for accessing Spotlight or alternative search tools.

Configuring Finder Window Defaults

- Open a new Finder window.

- Go to Finder Preferences.
- Under the General tab, find 'New Finder windows show.'
- Change the setting to 'New Finder windows show desktop.'

Now, when you open a new Finder window (Command+N), it will display your desktop by default. Customize this setting to your preference.

Configuring the Finder Sidebar

- Open Finder Preferences.
- Click on the Sidebar tab.

Customize your sidebar preferences:

- Check items like your home, pictures, music, and movies folders to have them appear under Favorites on the sidebar.
- Uncheck 'Recent' tags if you don't use tags to declutter the sidebar.

Feel free to configure the sidebar to your liking.

Adding 'Hard Disk' to Desktop

- In Finder Preferences, under the General tab, check 'Hard Disk' to display all internal and external disks on your desktop.

This makes it easy to access your disks directly from your desktop.

Keeping Folders on Top

- In Finder Preferences, go to the Advanced tab.
- Check 'Keep folders on top' for better organization when sorting by name.

This ensures that folders are displayed first, avoiding them getting mixed up with other items.

Customizing Search Behavior

- In Finder Preferences under the Advanced tab, adjust the 'When performing a search' setting using the drop-down menu to 'Search the current folder.'

This setting makes searches prioritize the folder you're currently in, enhancing efficiency.

Adding User Library to Sidebar

- In Finder, go to the Go menu.
- Hold the Option key to reveal the 'Library' destination, which is hidden by default.
- Click 'Library' to access your user library folder containing useful items like 'Application Support' and 'Preferences.'

To add it to the sidebar

- Go to the File menu and select 'Add to Sidebar' while in the 'Library' folder.

This provides quick access to your user library.

Enabling the Status Bar

- In Finder, go to the View menu.
- Select 'Show Status Bar' to display a status bar at the bottom of the Finder window, offering information on items, selection, and storage, along with an icon size slider in icon view.

Customizing Screenshots

- Use the keyboard shortcut Command+Shift+3 to take a screenshot.

- To eliminate the floating thumbnail preview, uncheck 'Show Floating Thumbnail' in the screenshot options.

This will make screenshots appear immediately on the desktop without a preview.

Disabling Screenshot Shadows

To remove shadows when taking screenshots of selected windows:

- Use the keyboard shortcut Command+Shift+4 to take a screenshot of a selected window.
- Hover over the window, press the Space bar, and click with the mouse.
- Disable the shadow by using the appropriate setting or option in your screenshot tool preferences.

This ensures that your window screenshots won't have shadows when used for tutorials or other purposes.

To remove shadows and convert screenshots to JPEG, you can use a terminal command. Follow these steps:

- Close the screenshot and open a TextEdit window.

- Paste the terminal command provided to eliminate the shadow and change the screenshot type to JPEG.
- Open a terminal window, paste the command, and press return to execute it.

Now, when you take a screenshot, it won't have the shadow. JPEG format is smaller and more suitable for web uploads.

Comparing File Sizes

By comparing the file sizes of screenshots, you'll notice a difference:

- Screenshot with shadow (PNG format): 771 kilobytes.
- Screenshot without shadow (JPEG format): 216 kilobytes.
- JPEG files are more compact, making them preferable for web use.

Using Stacks for a Tidy Desktop

- To keep your desktop organized, right-click on your desktop and select 'Use Stacks.' This groups similar files together and allows you to expand or compress stacks easily.

You can quick look the entire stack by selecting it and pressing the space bar. Additionally, you can scrub on a stack to view previews of each item within it, promoting a cleaner desktop.

Customizing Safari Start Page

Customize your Safari start page by clicking the settings button in the bottom right-hand corner. You can choose to display favorites, set a background image, or even use macOS wallpaper as your background. This personalized start page will appear each time you open a new window in Safari.

Enabling the Safari Status Bar

To enhance your browsing experience, open Safari, go to the 'View' menu, and select 'Show Status Bar.' This displays a status bar that provides previews of links and shows the URL when hovering over links.

Enabling the Develop Menu in Safari

To access the page source, enable the Develop menu in Safari. Follow these steps:

- In Safari, go to Preferences.
- Click on the Advanced tab.

- Enable 'Show Develop menu in menu bar.'

This will add a Develop menu to the menu bar, which includes the option to right-click and select 'Inspect Element' to view the page source.

Customizing the Dock

To customize your Dock, first, disable the Recent Applications section.

- Go to System Preferences > Dock & Menu Bar.
- Uncheck 'Show Recent Applications in Dock' to remove recent apps.
- When setting up your Mac for the first time, customize what's in the Dock.
- Remove default apps by dragging them up and letting go when you see 'Remove.'
- Trim the Dock to show only the apps you use regularly.

Keep apps in the Dock by:

- Right-click on the app icon.
- Go to Options.
- Select 'Keep in Dock' or drag the app to rearrange it in the Dock, which automatically keeps it there.

Resizing and Repositioning the Dock

Adjust the Dock size to fit your needs.

- Drag the vertical line in the Dock to make it larger or smaller.
- Alternatively, adjust it from System Preferences > Dock & Menu Bar.

Change the Dock's position on the screen.

- Go to System Preferences > Dock & Menu Bar.
- Under 'Position on screen,' choose left, right, or bottom.

Automatically Hide and Show Dock and Menu Bar

Hide the Dock and have it reappear when needed.

- Enable 'Automatically Hide and Show Dock' in System Preferences.
- The Dock will appear when you move your cursor to its location.
- Hide and show the menu bar for a cleaner desktop.
- Enable 'Automatically Hide and Show Menu Bar' in System Preferences.

The menu bar will appear when you move your cursor to the top of the screen.

Chapter 6: Important Settings You Need to Change

macOS Sonoma has more than 100 new features and changes, but it also includes several new settings that you probably did not even know about. So, in this chapter, I will show you settings that you need to change immediately after installing macOS Sonoma on your machine.

Change Your Wallpaper for Cool Animation

- Open your system settings.
- Navigate to the wallpaper section.
- Choose one of the New Motion wallpapers for a cool animation when locking and unlocking your device.
- Consider enabling wallpaper shuffling for a new one every day, every 12 hours, or continuously.
- To check how much space these wallpapers occupy, open Finder, go to "Go," then select "Folder."

- Enter the path: Library > Application Support > idle assets SD > customer.
- Look for '4K scr 240 FPS' and press Spacebar to see the space used.
- You can download or delete these wallpaper files to manage space.

Add Widgets to Your Desktop

- Go to system settings.
- Navigate to Desktop and Dock.
- Under the widgets section, choose to show widgets on the desktop.
- Customize widget style (full color, automatic grayscale) and enable/disable 'Use iPhone Widgets.'
- Select your preferred device for widget access.
- Adjust widget size by right-clicking and selecting the size you want.

Change Desktop Interaction Behavior

- Access system settings.
- Go to 'Desktop and Dock.'
- In the 'Desktop and Stage Manager' section, find 'click wallpaper to reveal desktop.'

- Change the setting to 'only in Stage Manager' if you don't want windows to disappear when clicking on the desktop.

Set Up Web Applications

- To create web app shortcuts, open a website like Google Docs.
- In the website's menu, select "File."
- Choose "Add to Dock" to create a web application.
- Customize the app's name, URL, and icon.
- Click "Add," and it will appear in your Dock as a separate application.
- You can edit web app URLs and appearance through settings.

Manage Game Mode

- When you open an application in full-screen mode, you may see the "Game Mode" option at the top.
- To turn off Game Mode, exit full screen by clicking the green icon.
- You can also enable or disable Game Mode from the game controller icon in the status bar.

Disable Pointer Acceleration for Gaming (Mouse)

- Access your settings.
- Navigate to the "Mouse" section and select "Advanced."
- Locate "Pointer Acceleration" and turn it off to improve gaming cursor speed.

Enable Auto-Switching for AirPods

- In your Bluetooth settings, find your AirPods.
- Ensure that "Connect to this Mac" is set to "automatically" to enable seamless switching between devices.

Turn Off Predictive Text

- Open system settings.
- Go to "Text Input" and select "Input Sources."
- Click "Edit" and disable "Show inline predictive text" if you don't want predictive text on macOS.

Customize Safari Profiles

- Access Safari settings and navigate to "Profiles."

- Create a new profile and explore additional settings.
- Customize favorites, new window preferences, and extensions for each profile.
- Adjust privacy and fingerprinting protection settings.
- Create custom keyboard shortcuts for profile-specific windows.

Clean Up Verification Codes

- In Safari settings, go to "Passwords."
- Enter your passcode and access "Password Options."
- Enable the option to auto-delete verification codes after autofill, ensuring a cleaner experience for two-factor authentication codes.

Share Passwords with Family

- In your system settings, navigate to the "Share passwords with family" option.
- To get started, create a shared group and add family members by name, email, or phone number.

- You can add passwords to this group and manage them collectively.
- Additionally, access password details by clicking the 'i' next to each password entry.

Adjust Video Effects for Video Calls

- To modify video effects during video calls, click on the purple icon in the status bar.
- Adjust portrait mode intensity and Studio Light effect.
- Enable or disable reactions and change microphone mode.
- If using Continuity Camera, choose between different camera lenses.

Customize Presenter Overlay in Video Calls

- When in a video call (e.g., Zoom or Google Meet), go to 'Share screen.'
- Access the purple icon in the status bar and enable 'Presenter Overlay.'

Choose between small or large overlay for an improved presentation experience.

Configure 'Hey Siri' Settings

- Access settings, then go to 'Siri and Spotlight.'
- Choose 'Listen for' and select between 'Siri,' 'Hey Siri,' or turn off the feature based on your preference.

Enhance Dictation Settings

- In system settings, navigate to 'Keyboard' and select 'Dictation.'
- Turn on dictation and experience improved functionality.
- Customize the dictation shortcut or specific key.
- Optionally, disable auto punctuation for manual control over punctuation marks during dictation.

Now you're all set to make these changes in macOS Sonoma.

Chapter 7: MacBook Pro Beginners Guide

First, select the language. Make sure to choose English for the language. Next, select your country or region. Now, pick an appearance for your Mac: you can go for the light mode, dark mode, or set it to Auto. Light mode keeps your machine bright all day long, while auto mode switches between light and dark modes as the sun sets.

Apple devices come packed with accessibility features. For those with visual impairments, there's an option to reduce motion on the screen. You can customize your keyboard for accessibility. Under the hearing section, you can enable closed captions and flash alerts to get your attention.

"Speak selection" is a helpful feature. It reads selected text when you press the option and Escape keys. "Typing feedback" speaks characters, words, and selection changes as you type. Another option is "hover text," which enlarges text under the pointer. These features make your Mac more accessible.

Now, set up your Wi-Fi network. Don't forget to enter your password. If there's a software update available, we recommend installing it. This is crucial if you're using advanced data protection or security keys from Apple. The update may take a few minutes, during which the system will download and install it over Wi-Fi.

One accessibility feature you might want to enable is Zoom. Keep an eye out for the data and privacy icon; it appears when Apple needs your personal information.

If you're transferring data from another Mac, a Time Machine backup, a startup disk, or a Windows PC, the Migration Assistant is there to assist.

Now, sign in with your Apple ID. This allows you to access services like iCloud and the App Store. If you have two-factor authentication enabled, verify your identity with your security key or a six-digit verification code. Once that's done, you'll be asked to accept the terms and conditions.

With your Apple ID set, it's time to create your computer account. Provide your account name and password. If you're setting up an account via iCloud, you might need to verify it with your iPhone password. Once that's done, your Mac will sync settings from your iPhone.

Some important settings

You can customize location services, device analytics, app analytics, Siri, screen time, and appearance. In the lower left, there's the option for "12V disk encryption" for added file security. Next up is Touch ID, which uses your fingerprint to unlock your Mac. Simply place your finger on the sensor a few times to register it. Lastly, you can set up Apple Pay for convenient transactions.

Your desktop will display your folders and any other files or icons you add. At the bottom, you'll find the dock, which houses your most frequently used applications. You can easily add or remove apps from the dock to suit your preferences.

In the top left corner, you'll see the Apple logo and menu options. These menus will change based on the application you're using. For instance, in Finder, the menus will be file-related. The top right corner shows the time, Control Center, and menu icons.

Applications

When you open the applications folder, you'll see all the installed apps on your Mac. Another way to access them is through the Launchpad on the dock. To copy and paste items within the file system, you can use the keyboard shortcuts Command-C and Command-V, or simply use the file menu options at the top of the screen.

To open an application, just click its icon. To close it, either use Command-Q or navigate to the application name in the menu bar and select "Quit." In the dock, open apps have a dot beneath them. You can also right-click to quit them. For unresponsive apps, force quit is an option. Hold down Command-Option-Escape, select the misbehaving app, and click "Force Quit."

When it comes to installing applications on your Mac, there are several convenient methods at your disposal. The easiest is using the Mac App Store. Simply scroll through and find the application you want, then click "Install." You'll be prompted to enter your Apple ID login information. If you've recently set up your Mac, it may ask if you'd like to use Touch ID for future purchases. If you agree, future installations will authenticate with Touch ID rather than a password.

With a few clicks, you've successfully installed a new application. You'll notice the Launchpad icon jumping, and you can access the app from there or find it in the Finder's Applications folder. The Mac App Store simplifies the process—just log in with your Apple ID and download or purchase any Mac app you need.

For applications not available on the Mac App Store, clicking "Download" typically yields a .DMG disk image file. Once you open the .DMG, you can drag the application to the Applications folder. If you already have it installed, you'll be asked whether you want to keep both versions or replace the existing one. Alternatively, some apps can be installed simply by clicking the installation file, which will download and install the latest version, extracting the app and opening it. Regardless of how you install an app, they all end up in your Applications folder.

After installing an app using a .DMG file, you can eject it by dragging it to the trash, and then you can delete the DMG file from your Downloads folder.

Another quick and efficient way to open applications is using Spotlight. Hold down Command-Spacebar to activate Spotlight search, where you can find files, apps, initiate web searches, or perform calculations. Spotlight is a speedy way to access your applications—just hold Command-Spacebar, type the app's name, and hit Open or Enter. To close an app, click and hold its icon in the dock and select "Quit."

How to update your computer

- Go to System Preferences, then General, and click on Software Update.

It's crucial to check for software updates as soon as you set up your computer. You can also visit the Mac App Store and head to "Updates" to find available application updates. Make sure you keep both your operating system and applications up to date to ensure optimal performance.

How to change your desktop wallpaper

Simply control-click on your desktop and choose "Change Wallpaper" to access System Preferences. If you prefer, you can go directly to System Preferences through the dock or by clicking the Apple logo. In System Preferences, select "Wallpaper." The easiest way is to control-click on your desktop and choose "Change Wallpaper." You can change your wallpaper by selecting different options, and the changes will appear in real time. macOS offers various themes that match both light and dark mode, as well as the option to use photos or files from your computer.

macOS allows you to have multiple desktops, and you can set different wallpapers for each one. You can access these desktops by using Mission Control, either through the Mission Control option or a four-finger swipe-up gesture. In Mission Control, you can add or remove desktops and set individual wallpapers for each. It's a great way to keep things organized and visually appealing.

You can also assign applications to specific desktops. Right-click on an app in the dock, go to "Options," and select "Assign to Desktop." This ensures that the app opens on the designated desktop of your choice.

Another neat feature is setting an application to open at login. To do this, hold down on the app in the dock, go to "Options," and choose "Open at Login." Now, that application will automatically launch every time you log into your computer. This can be done for any app in the dock by simply right-clicking on it, navigating to "Options," and selecting "Open at Login." It's a useful way to have your most-used apps ready when you start your computer.

Remove an application from the dock

If you ever want to remove an application from the dock, it's quite simple. You can either hold down the Option key and click "Remove from Dock," or just click and hold the application icon, drag it out of the dock, and release it. If you change your mind and wish to add the application back, it's just as easy. You can drag it back into the dock, and it'll be readily accessible again.

If you'd like to customize the position and orientation of the dock on your screen, you can do so by going to System Preferences, then Desktop and Dock. The dock typically rests at the bottom, but you can choose to move it to the left or right, depending on your preference. In the same menu, you can enable the option to automatically hide and show the dock. When enabled, the dock disappears when you're not using it, offering more screen real estate. To access it, simply move your mouse to the very bottom of the screen, and it will reappear. This is especially handy if you want to maximize your available workspace and only reveal the dock when you need it.

When you take an application into full-screen mode, you might notice that the menu bar at the top disappears. You can control this behavior by setting it to automatically hide in full-screen mode or to always remain visible. It's up to you to decide which suits your workflow better.

Hot corners

Another nifty feature in macOS, accessible through System Preferences under Desktop and Dock, is "hot corners." By default, one of these hot corners is designated for Quick Note. You can customize these corners to perform various actions. For instance, you can make the top right corner activate Mission Control, the top left corner show the desktop, or the bottom left corner reveal application windows. After configuring your hot corners, you can easily access these actions by moving your mouse cursor to the designated corner of the screen. It's a convenient way to streamline your Mac experience.

In macOS, under System Preferences, you'll find the "Internet Accounts" option. Here, you can add various internet accounts such as iCloud, Google, and Microsoft

Exchange. When you add an account, it automatically syncs with macOS default apps like Contacts, Notes, and Mail. This way, all your data is readily available and interconnected.

Another notable feature in macOS is "Stacks." This handy tool automatically groups similar files together, keeping your desktop clean and organized. It can group multiple files of the same type, such as screenshots or PDFs, for easier access. You can enable Stacks by right-clicking and selecting "Use Stacks." This helps you keep your desktop clutter-free and makes it more efficient to access your files.

Notification Center Customization

One of the handy features in macOS is the Notification Center. It's super easy to access. Just click on the time in the upper right corner, and voila! You have access to all sorts of widgets. You can even personalize it by adding widgets that suit your needs. Just click on 'Edit Widgets' at the bottom, and you'll see a list of widgets you can add. You can drag and drop them to your heart's content, making your Notification Center your very own.

Clock Customization

You can also customize your clock in macOS. Go to 'System Preferences,' navigate to 'Control Center,' scroll down to 'menu bar only,' and select 'Clock.' Here, you can tweak your clock settings to match your preferences. Whether you prefer a digital or analog clock, a 24-hour or AM/PM display, or even time separators, it's all up to you. You can even enable the 'Announce Time on the half-hour' feature to stay on track.

Window Management

Managing windows in macOS is a breeze. You can easily enter full-screen mode or split your screen in various ways. You can do this by holding down the green icon on the window and choosing your desired option. Alternatively, try dragging one application on top of another in Mission Control to put them side by side. It's a super cool way to multitask.

Stage Manager for Application Organization

If you're someone who juggles many applications at once, you'll love Stage Manager. Access it through the Control Center in the menu bar. It organizes your open apps by their names, so you can swiftly switch between them. Say goodbye to window clutter and hello to an organized workspace.

Safari and Finder Tabs

Both Safari and Finder have tabs for better organization. In Safari, you can merge all open windows into one for a neater browsing experience. In Finder, you can open new tabs with a quick keyboard shortcut (Command + T). This way, you can work between multiple locations with ease and even drag and drop files between tabs.

Managing Trash and Downloads

Don't forget to clear your Trash regularly to keep your Mac tidy. You can right-click on items in the Trash and select 'Put Back' if you want to restore them. Or, if you're sure you want to permanently erase everything, just click 'Empty.' It's a satisfying way to declutter your computer.

Speaking of clutter, your Downloads folder can quickly fill up. Make it a habit to move unused items to the Trash and empty it regularly. This will help keep your Mac running smoothly.

These features in macOS can streamline your experience and make your Mac work better for you. So go ahead and explore, customize, and organize to make the most of your Mac!

How to Screen Record on Mac

Begin by clicking on the magnifying glass at the top right of your Mac to open Spotlight search.

- In Spotlight search, type "QuickTime Player" and select it from the results.
- If nothing appears when you initially tap on QuickTime, don't worry; just press Cancel.
- Alternatively, find QuickTime in your Dock at the bottom and open it by clicking with two fingers.
- Inside QuickTime Player, look for "New Screen Recording" and tap on it. This will open a bar at the bottom, offering different recording options.
- Choose whether to record your entire screen or a selected portion of it.
- For more customization, click on "Options" to explore settings like where to save the recording or your microphone source.

Start Recording

- Initiate the recording by tapping "Record."
- To stop recording, go to the top right of your Mac and click on the stop button (a circle with a square inside).
- After stopping, the screen recording video will open, allowing you to review the recorded content.

Saving or Exporting

- To save or export your recording for later use, access the "File" option at the top right of your Mac.
- Select either "Export As" or "Save," and configure your preferences such as resolution and destination.

Wait for the recording to be saved; it won't take long for a short video. Once saved, you can access it on your desktop. Double-tap to watch the recording or share it with others or edit as needed.

Chapter 8: Troubleshooting

macOS Sonoma Desktop Widgets Not Working on Mac

Unfortunately, some Mac OS Sonoma users are facing issues with these widgets.

First, make sure the widgets can access your location:

- Go to System Settings.
- Click on Privacy and Security.
- Then select Location Services.
- Ensure the toggles for the affected apps are enabled.

Next, consider removing and re-adding the widgets:

- Right-click on the widget and choose Remove Widget.
- Click on the time at the top-right corner, then hit Edit Widgets.
- Find the Reddit widget, select the size, and drag it to the desktop.

Ensure your Mac can use iPhone widgets:

- In System Settings, go to Desktop and Dock.
- Scroll down to the Region section and enable the toggle for Use iPhone widgets.

If the issue persists, restart your Mac:

- Click on the Apple menu at the top-left and choose Restart.

Finally, update your Mac's software to fix any hidden bugs:

- Open System Settings.
- Click on General.
- Select Software Update and download/install the latest macOS update.

These steps should help you resolve the issues on your Mac. Your widgets should be working smoothly now.

MacBook Camera Not Working

First, make sure your Mac's camera is working properly.

- Open the Safari browser on your Mac and type "webcam test" in the search bar.
- Open the first website, then click on "test my cam" and allow the camera to be used.

So, you have checked the camera, and the camera is fine. Now, what you need to do is:

- Go to the Apple logo and click on "Force Quit."
- After that, all the applications that are running in the background, force quit all of them.

Then, see if your camera works or not.

If this solution doesn't work and your camera doesn't turn on, then try the third method by going to "Settings."

- Scroll down and find "Privacy and Security," and click on it.
- Now, find the camera on the right side and click on it.
- Here, make sure that the app you want to use the camera is turned on.
- If the apps are not turned on, they won't be able to use the camera. So, turn on the camera from here.

macOS Sonoma Not Updating

First, let's get your Mac upgraded to Mac OS Sonoma.

- Go to "General" settings and select "Software Update." If you don't see the Sonoma update, make sure your MacBook, iMac, or Mac Mini is compatible with Sonoma. Check the list of supported devices.

If your device is compatible but you're facing issues with downloading or installing Sonoma, check for any pending updates that may interfere with the process.

- Scroll to the bottom of the "Software Update" page and click on "More Info" under "Other Updates Available."
- Install any pending updates, then retry upgrading to Sonoma.
- Ensure your device has enough free storage, more than what the update requires.
- Turn off "Lockdown Mode," as it can interfere with the upgrade.
- If you have a MacBook, it should have more than 50% battery or be connected to a charger.

If you encounter errors during installation or download, or if your Mac can't check for updates, ensure your device is connected to a stable internet connection.

- Check your network speed; if it's slow, switch to a better network.
- If the "update" button is unresponsive, restart your Mac and try the update again.

After making sure of all these steps, attempt downloading Mac Sonoma again.

macOS Sonoma Bluetooth Issues

Bluetooth problems in Sonoma can include:

- Devices not pairing with your Mac.
- Audible interference or glitching when using Bluetooth headphones or speakers.
- Issues with Bluetooth keyboards or mice, such as typing errors or erratic mouse movement.

These problems may result from software conflicts, low battery, interference, or damaged Bluetooth modules. Regular maintenance can help prevent and resolve these issues.

Steps to Fix Mac OS Sonoma Bluetooth Problems

- Restarting your Mac can often resolve issues.

Check for Updates

- Go to system settings > General > Software Update and install any available updates.

Troubleshoot Individual Devices

If the issue involves a single device:

- Ensure it's fully charged or has fresh batteries.
- Try turning it off and on.
- These steps can resolve problems related to low power.

If the problem affects multiple devices:

- Turn off Bluetooth on your Mac and then turn it back on.
- This can resolve connectivity issues.

Disconnect and Reconnect Devices

- If simply reconnecting doesn't work, unpair and pair the device again:
- Click on Control Center, then Bluetooth.
- Click the device to disconnect it and click again to reconnect.
- Alternatively, go to the Bluetooth section in system settings, disconnect, and reconnect.

Unpair Devices Completely

- In system settings > Bluetooth:
- Click the "i" next to the device's name.
- Choose "Forget this device."
- Follow the device's manual to pair it again.

Remove Interference

Address interference issues by:

- Moving your Mac away from other electrical equipment or power sources.
- Switching 2.4 GHz Wi-Fi devices to 5 GHz if possible.
- Ensure there are no obstacles between your Mac and the device.

Disconnect USB or Thunderbolt Devices

- As a last resort, disconnect any USB or Thunderbolt devices from your Mac to eliminate potential conflicts.

Reset the Mac's Bluetooth Module

If none of the previous steps work, you can reset the Mac's Bluetooth module:

- Go to Applications > Utilities and launch Terminal.

- Type sudo pkill BluetoothD and press return.
- Enter your password if prompted.
- Quit Terminal and restart your Mac.

Following these steps should help you resolve Mac OS Sonoma Bluetooth issues and enjoy a smoother user experience.

macOS Sonoma Draining Your Battery

Have you upgraded to Mac OS Sonoma and noticed that your Mac's battery drains more quickly than before?

One way to reduce battery drain is by freeing up RAM. If you own a recent Mac with 8 GB of RAM, you might notice it fills up quickly. When this happens, your Mac resorts to using your startup disk as virtual RAM, which is slower and more energy-intensive.

Sonoma is more demanding of your Mac's resources (CPU, GPU, and RAM) compared to Ventura, which could contribute to faster battery drain, particularly if your Mac isn't plugged in. If your battery is draining significantly faster after upgrading to Sonoma, consider the following factors:

- Spotlight may be reindexing. Check for indexing by clicking on the Spotlight icon in the menu bar.

- Photos might be syncing. Look for a status message at the bottom of the Photos window.
- Ensure Time Machine isn't backing up your Mac. Access this by clicking on The Time Machine menu.
- Check for app updates by clicking on Launchpad in the dock.

If none of the mentioned factors is causing the battery drain, use Activity Monitor to further investigate:

- Navigate to your Applications folder, then Utilities, and launch Activity Monitor.
- Click the top of the percent CPU column to order processes by CPU cycles. If any process uses a significant percentage, select it and click the X in the toolbar.
- If needed, repeat the same process for the percentage GPU column.

To reduce battery drain, consider these strategies:

- Close unnecessary browser tabs.
- Quit applications you're not currently using.
- Keep your applications updated.
- Activate low power mode in System Settings > Battery.

- If your Mac's fans are working hard due to overheating, find a cooler environment, if possible, to alleviate the strain on your Mac.

Lastly, some applications launch automatically at startup and might contribute to battery drain. To manage them:

- If you identify unnecessary items, disable them to potentially resolve battery drain issues.

By following these steps, you can better understand and address the causes of battery drain in Mac OS Sonoma. This will help you determine if it's due to the new operating system's demands or another underlying issue, and provide you with practical solutions.

No Internet After Upgrade

- Open "System Settings."
- Select "Network."
- Then, choose "VPN & Filters."
- In the "Filters & Proxies" section, change the status for "Little Snitch" from "Enabled" to "Disabled."

Now, you have Internet access. However, please note that the issue is caused by having an outdated version of

Little Snitch installed. The problem stems from using an outdated version of Little Snitch, which is not compatible with the new Sonoma operating system. To resolve this issue, you need to upgrade your Little Snitch to a compatible version, and everything will function correctly.

Wi-Fi Problems on macOS Sonoma

Many Mac applications require an internet connection, which typically means using Wi-Fi. If your Wi-Fi isn't working correctly, it's a significant issue.

To begin, determine what's causing the issue. If it only affects a single application, the problem might lie with that specific app. If it's isolated to your Mac and not other devices on your Wi-Fi network, the issue may be with your Mac. However, if it's impacting all devices on your Wi-Fi network, the culprit could be your router or broadband provider.

The simplest Wi-Fi issues to address are those that affect just one application. To verify this, open another web browser and check if it connects. If it does, the issue likely stems from the troubled application. For example, Chrome often encounters page-loading problems. To fix application-specific problems, start by restarting the app. If that doesn't work, and it's a web browser, you can try clearing the browser's cache, typically found in the browser's privacy and security settings.

If the Wi-Fi issues extend beyond a single application, proceed to the next step, which is turning off and then on your Mac's Wi-Fi. This classic advice is effective.

- Click the Wi-Fi icon in the menu bar or in the control center, toggle Wi-Fi off, wait a few seconds, and then toggle it on again.
- If this doesn't resolve the issue, reboot your Mac.

Restarting can often resolve various problems by clearing temporary files and performing checks on your startup disk.

If none of the previous steps have worked, check if your phone or tablet can connect to Wi-Fi and the internet. If not, the issue likely lies with your Wi-Fi router or your broadband provider's network. Ensure the cable between your router and the broadband socket is securely connected.

- Restart your router and allow it to reset.

If problems persist, consider moving your router away from walls, ceilings, or electrical equipment. If issues persist, contact your broadband provider to inquire about any network faults in your area.

If other devices work while your Mac doesn't, continue troubleshooting on your Mac. Here are a few more steps to try:

- Clear the DNS cache. DNS, or Domain Name Service, matches web addresses with IP addresses. Sometimes, the cache storing this data can get corrupted.
- If clearing the DNS cache doesn't work, the issue might be with your service provider's DNS server. To test this, switch to Google's DNS servers in your system settings.

If the problem still persists, try renewing the DHCP lease. DHCP is the system used by your router to allocate an IP address to your Mac. Without a proper IP address, your Mac can't connect to the internet. To renew the DHCP lease:

- navigate to system settings,
- select Wi-Fi, click on the "I" icon,
- choose TCP/IP, and click "Renew DHCP Lease."

If none of the above steps resolve the issue, the final option is to consider reinstalling Mac OS Sonoma. You can do this by restarting your Mac in recovery mode and choosing the "Reinstall Mac OS Sonoma" option from the menu.

MacBook Screen Flickering

It's not like every Max screen flickers, but if it is happening, we are here to help you. This issue could be due to compatibility issues with Mac OS or Graphics Processing Unit. But not to worry, here are the best fixes:

- Fix #1: Restart your Mac. Click the Apple icon from the left corner and choose restart. Many problems can be resolved immediately. If it still flickers, consider updating your Mac OS. You can do this by clicking the Apple icon, going to system preferences, and clicking software update.
- Fix #2: Clear cache and system junk. This is an essential step because cleaning old junk, cache, and temporary files can resolve numerous issues that slow down your system. Your machine will run smoothly. For this step, we recommend downloading "Clean Up My System," which offers a

cache cleaner, junk cleaner, and trash cleaner in separate tabs. Click Start to automatically clear out redundant files in the system.

- Fix #3: Reset your PRAM (Parameter Random Access Memory), which deals with the display parameters of your Mac. To do this, follow these steps:
    - Click on the Apple icon and shut down your Mac completely.
    - When you turn it on, press command option P and R keys for about 20 seconds. Release them when the system starts.
- Fix #4: Adjust energy saver settings. Open system preferences and go to energy saver. Uncheck "Automatic Graphic Switching" to prevent the system from switching between two graphic cards and causing flickering issues.
- Fix #5: Disable True Tone. For this, go to system preferences and click on "Display." Uncheck the True Tone box.

One of these fixes will help you resolve the flickering issue.

Fixing Keyboard and Trackpad Issues on MacBook Pro

Experiencing problems with your MacBook Pro's keyboard and trackpad not working can be frustrating. Here, I'll guide you through the solutions.

Identifying the Issue

If your MacBook Pro's keyboard suddenly stops working, several reasons could be behind it. These include software glitches, outdated operating systems, hardware issues like loose connections or damage, and even unexpected spills or dust accumulation. Ensure your device is updated, clean, and safe from harm.

Non-Responsive Keyboard

If your MacBook Pro's keyboard isn't typing, it could be a software glitch or hardware malfunction. Start with a device restart or reset the System Management Controller (SMC). For hardware problems, consider consulting an Apple technician.

Keyboard and Trackpad Not Working After Login

If your keyboard and trackpad work during login but fail afterward, a software issue is likely. You can try booting your MacBook in safe mode. This will load only essential system software and may help identify software conflicts causing the problem.

- Navigate to the Apple menu.
- Click "Shutdown."
- After the device shuts down, press the power button until you see "Loading Startup Options."
- Choose your volume option (usually Macintosh HD) and, while pressing the shift key, select the option to continue in safe mode.
- Your system will restart, and you'll see "Safe Boot" displayed on the menu bar. Check if your keyboard and trackpad are working now.

Resetting SMC and NVRAM

Resetting the Parameter RAM (PRAM) and Non-Volatile RAM (NVRAM) can help in some cases. PRAM stores settings such as speaker volume, screen resolution, and startup disk selection. NVRAM stores settings your Mac accesses quickly.

Keyboard and Trackpad Issues After Sleep

If your keyboard and trackpad stop working after your MacBook wakes up, consider checking power management settings or minor software glitches. An SMC reset can often resolve these problems.

For issues where the power button works, but the keyboard and trackpad don't, start with basic troubleshooting, like a device restart or a PRAM reset.

Resolving Issues After a Spill

If your MacBook gets wet, immediately turn it off and unplug connected devices to prevent short circuits. Gently blot (not wipe) spilled liquid with an absorbent cloth. Afterward, cautiously attempt to turn your MacBook Pro back on. If the keyboard and trackpad are still unresponsive or show irregularities, seek professional help.

Post-Battery Replacement Issues

Replacement procedures can sometimes disrupt internal connections. If you encounter issues after a battery replacement, it's possible that the keyboard and trackpad connectors have become loose or damaged. Consider revisiting your technician for a check-up.

Fixing an Unresponsive Trackpad

If your MacBook Pro's trackpad doesn't respond, start by ensuring it's not an environmental issue. Dust, liquid spills, or temperature changes can affect the trackpad's sensitivity. Clean it gently with a microfiber cloth.

- Boot your MacBook in safe mode. This will trigger a disk check and clear caches, potentially resolving trackpad issues.
- Reset the SMC and PRAM/NVRAM, as these settings can affect trackpad functionality.

Remember, both software and hardware issues can cause keyboard and trackpad problems. Start with basic troubleshooting and, if issues persist, consult with a professional. Regular maintenance and care can prevent many of these issues.

Most Common macOS Sonoma Issues and Fixes

Before we dive into Sonoma issues, there's one crucial step you must take: back up your Mac. Regular backups are essential, but they are especially critical before installing a new OS like Mac OS Sonoma. Failing to do so could result in data loss. It's recommended to use Time Machine for this purpose. It will make restoration easy if you decide to roll back to Ventura or need to reinstall Sonoma.

If your Mac is not on the compatibility list, you might encounter issues installing Sonoma. The following Mac models are compatible with Mac OS Sonoma:

- iMac 2019 and later
- Mac Pro 2019 and later
- iMac Pro 2017
- Mac Studio 2022 and later
- MacBook Air 2018 and later
- Mac Mini 2018 and later
- MacBook Pro 2018 and later

To check if Sonoma is downloading correctly, you should verify your internet connection and Apple's server status. Apple provides a status page for its services, including update services. Check for the Sonoma upgrade server's status. If it's green, there's nothing wrong with your connection or Apple's servers. If it's red, you'll need to wait for it to be fixed.

If Sonoma downloads but fails to install, try rebooting your Mac in safe mode. For Intel Macs, hold down the Shift key, and for Apple Silicon Macs, hold down the power button. Then attempt the installation again.

After updating to Sonoma, you might notice that your Mac is running slower. This is due to the increased demands on your Mac's resources. To address this, follow these steps:

- Update applications.
- Clear out unnecessary files.
- Free up RAM.
- Run maintenance scripts.
- Manage login items and launch agents.
- Close unused browser tabs.
- Quit applications that you're not using.

If you experience app crashes after updating to Sonoma, follow these steps:

- Ensure your apps are up to date.
- Check with the app developer to confirm compatibility with Sonoma.
- If the app is compatible, consider reinstalling it.

In the rare case that you encounter issues with Bluetooth or Wi-Fi after the update, follow these steps:

- Toggle Bluetooth or Wi-Fi off and then back on through the Control Center in the menu bar.
- If the issue persists, use the Wi-Fi Diagnostics tool by Option-clicking the Wi-Fi menu. For

Bluetooth, unpair and then repair the problematic device.

These are the main issues you might face after upgrading to Mac OS Sonoma. Follow these instructions to address them. If all else fails, as a last resort, you can boot into recovery mode and reinstall Sonoma. Alternatively, you can restore from your Time Machine backup to revert to Ventura if you no longer wish to use Sonoma.

Conclusion

macOS Sonoma has officially arrived and this update is packed with fantastic additions, and screen savers are just the beginning. The new feature allows you to select stunning locations from around the world, seamlessly transitioning from your lock screen wallpaper to your desktop wallpaper. It's a visually appealing effect that creates a cohesive and pleasing look. You can also shuffle through various themes, including landscapes, cityscapes, underwater scenes, and Earth views. Gone are the days of lackluster macOS screensavers; this update gives them a fresh and captivating twist, making you want to transition between your lock and home screens just to savor the experience.

The ability to place widgets directly on your desktop is a game-changer. It's probably one of the most practical uses of widgets I've seen. You have the freedom to position them wherever you like, making them more versatile than on iPadOS or iOS. What's even more impressive is that these widgets adapt to the color of your wallpaper, providing a seamless integration. They're not just static; you can interact with them, checking off tasks and launching applications directly from the desktop. Plus, if you're an iPhone user, you can add iOS widgets to your Mac when your iPhone is nearby or on the same Wi-Fi network, offering a unique and unified experience.

macOS Sonoma introduces some exciting additions that work not only with FaceTime but also third-party video conferencing apps like Zoom. One standout feature is the presenter overlay, which keeps you front and center while sharing your screen. It's perfect for giving presentations during Zoom or FaceTime calls, creating an engaging and professional experience. Additionally, you'll find a range of new camera effects, such as hearts, balloons, and confetti, to add a bit of fun to your work calls.

For gamers, Apple is taking Mac gaming to the next level with a new game mode. This mode prioritizes CPU and GPU resources, resulting in more consistent frame rates and reduced latency for wireless controllers and AirPods. It's a significant upgrade, especially if you enjoy gaming on your Mac, even if you have a non-Pro machine like a MacBook Air. Apple silicon is the driving force behind this, putting gaming performance at the forefront.

macOS Sonoma is here to elevate your Mac experience with these new and impressive features. From stunning screen savers to versatile widgets, enhanced video call capabilities, improved gaming performance, and an organized browsing experience, this update has something for everyone. Give it a try and discover the difference for yourself.

Good luck!

Made in United States
North Haven, CT
13 November 2023